The Printing Press

GREAT INVENTIONS

The Printing Press

MILTON MELTZER

BENCHMARK BOOKS

MARSHALL CAVENDISH
NEW YORK

Benchmark Books
Marshall Cavendish
99 White Plains Road
Tarrytown, NY 10591-9001
www.marshallcavendish.com
Copyright © 2004 by Milton Meltzer

All Internet sites were available and accurate when sent to press.

Library of Congress Cataloging-in-Publication Data

Meltzer, Milton, 1915–
The printing press / by Milton Meltzer.
p. cm. — (Great inventions)
Summary: Explains the mechanics of the first printing press, invented in
Germany by Gutenberg in the fifteenth century, and describes the press's
revolutionary impact on the world.
Includes bibliographical references and index.
ISBN 0-7614-1536-X
1. Printing—History—Juvenile literature. 2.
Printing—History—Origin and antecedents—Juvenile literature. 3.
Printing presses—Juvenile literature. [1. Printing—History. 2.
Printing presses.] I. Title. II. Series: Great inventions (Benchmark
Books (Firm))

Z124 .M496 2003
686.2—dc21
2002015307

Photo research by Candlepants, Inc.

Series Design by Sonia Chaghatzbanian

Cover Photo: Galleria d' Arte Moderna Rome/ Dagli Orti/Art Archive

The photographs in this book are used by permission and through the courtesy of: *Art Archive*:Gal-leria d' Arte Moderna Rome/ Dagli Orti, 2; Galleria degli Uffizi Flobence/Dagli Orti (A), 46, Eileen Tweedy, 66; Bibliotheque des Arts Dcoratifs Paris/Dagli Orti, 48; Muse des Beaux Arts D'le/Dagli Orti, 60; Dagli Orti, 62; *Corbis*: Francis G. Mayer, 10; Gianni Dagli Orti, 13; Charles & Josette Lenars, 15; Historical Picture Archive, 19, 50; Bettmann, 20, 26, 34, 36, 42, 52, 56, 58, 76, 79, 81, 82, 84–85, 88, 92, 96, 99, 101, 102, 104,107, 108; Archivo Iconografico, 24–25, 30, 64, 73; Ali Mewyer, 28; Enzo & Paulo Ragazzini, 68; The Corcoran Gallery of Art, Washington DC, 90; Corbis, 32, 40, 87, 94; *Art Resource, NY*: Erich Lessing, 12; Réunion des Musées Nationaux, 27, 70; Fo-toteca Internacional Lda, 38, 7475; The Pierpont Morgan Library, 44; Scala, 53.

Printed in China

1 3 5 6 4 2

CONTENTS

Foreword		9
One	Speaking, Writing, and Reading	11
Two	Scribes and Scrolls	18
Three	Was China First?	26
Four	How Gutenberg Did It	33
Five	Printing, Printing, Everywhere	41
Six	The Print Shop: A Cultural Center	49
Seven	From Apprentice to Master	59
Eight	An Aid to Science	67
Nine	From Luther to Plymouth Rock	75
Ten	The Printing Press and Democracy	78
Eleven	Many Voices	84
Twelve	In Love with the Printed Word	91
Thirteen	The Power of Print	98
Fourteen	The New Place of Print	105
Afterword		111
Web Sites		113
Bibliography		115
Index		119

The Printing Press

How do we know what we know? Our minds are full of stuff—facts, ideas, stories, gossip, names, memories—good stuff and bad. Stuff that we believe in, stuff that we don't.

Where does it all come from?

We absorb it from the world around us. What others tell us: family, friends, neighbors, schoolmates, teachers. What we see and hear on the radio and television, and in the movies. And what, in this modern information age, we get from the Internet, through search engines and e-mail and e-books.

But much of what we take into our heads still comes from the printed word. Print, print, everywhere—in newspapers, magazines, leaflets, posters, billboards, and especially books.

Printing: that is what this book is about. How the process of printing was invented, and the multiple effects the invention has had on our lives and our world in the more than five hundred years since.

Does it matter? Some historians believe that the invention of printing technology was a unique event central to the history of mankind because it signaled not only the end of the Middle Ages, but the beginning of the modern world. Science itself, some believe, was unthinkable without the information that printing provided. No invention, it has been said, stirred people's imaginations quite as much as the invention of printing.

One of the cave paintings at Lascaux in southern France, discovered by chance in 1940. Created during the most recent ice age, it dates back to around 14000 to 13500 B.C.

Speaking, Writing, and Reading

Many think that the ability of humans to speak separates us from all others and makes us superior. The ability to put that communication into writing was an even greater advance in the development of civilization. Now we could tell one another what we had in mind in situations where the other person was not present. The written message allowed this. Even more: writing enabled us to preserve communications, or records, from the past. It marked the beginning of recorded history.

Then, long, long after, came the invention of printing as a means of communication. It is often said that Johann Gutenberg of the German city of Mainz invented the printing press around 1450. But credit for the technique of printing, as for almost any invention, needs to be given to a number of people, most of whose names are unknown to us.

The basic idea of printing is the reproduction of images that the eye can see on a surface such as paper. There are a great number and variety of printing products, but all can be seen and are produced in quantities ranging from one to millions.

From the time of the earliest humans, people have tried to create images of their lives and the world in which they lived. Think of the Paleolithic period (the Old Stone Age), the earliest period of human

SCRIBES IN ANCIENT EGYPT, USING REED PENS, RECORD THE HARVEST ON SHEETS OF PAPYRUS.
THIS DETAIL IS OF A WALL PAINTING IN THE TOMB OF A GOVERNMENT INSPECTOR.

THIS CLAY TABLET, USING WEDGE-SHAPED CHARACTERS TO RECORD THE NUMBER OF SHEEP AND GOATS, IS AN EXAMPLE OF THE CUNEIFORM WRITING OF THE SUMERIAN PEOPLE IN ANCIENT MESOPOTAMIA. IT DATES TO AROUND 2350 B.C.

development. It began about 2 million years ago and ended in some parts of the world between 40,000 and 10,000 years ago. Perhaps you have read about the magnificent paintings on the walls or ceilings of caves at Altamira, Spain (discovered in 1879), and at Lascaux in the Dordogne region of France (found in 1940). Lascaux dates back 15,000 years, Altamira even further. Using a variety of techniques, the Cro-Magnon people created mostly animal but also some human figures that are masterworks of prehistoric art. Such rock carving and painting have been found in other parts of the world as well.

It was in the ancient Middle East, in Mesopotamia and Egypt, that the first writing appeared, scholars believe. As those agricultural societies became more complex, the need for people to communicate with each other in some sort of recorded form stimulated invention. In speech the use of articulate sounds enables us to exchange ideas, wishes, and questions with other people. Writing builds on the same foundation, using visual instead of audible signs. The signs used in the ancient Middle East were pictures. Their shapes designated real things, such as animals, plants, weapons, buildings, tools, furniture, people, and gods.

It seems likely that a major motive for inventing writing was commercial. If you wanted to remember that a certain number of sheep belonged to a specific family, then you wrote it down. Or suppose you wanted to know that those sheep were being herded for sale to someone in a particular place. A written sign served as an aid to memory. A picture of the sheep's head stood for the animal, so that someone reading it knew the business deal was in sheep. Notches or scratches indicated quantity, and perhaps some other pictogram denoted the names of the buyer and seller.

Yet there were limits. It was not hard to draw a horse or a man when you wanted to write about a horse or a man. But how could you express abstract ideas such as "to love," or "to be sad," or "to think"? Eventually people figured out that they could use signs, not for what they picture, but for their phonetic values and their sounds. The standard of writing became phonemic. That is, it tried to symbolize all of the significant sounds of the language. When the goal of one letter for one sound was reached, you had a complete alphabet.

Early writing was often inscribed on clay tablets. That made it more permanent. By using tablets, you could store and retrieve far more information than you could by holding it in memory.

While those first writers were making marks on clay, creating a new art, another art was being created to make meaning out of it—the art of reading. The writer set down a message; the reader deciphered it.

It sounds easy because we take reading and writing for granted. They seem such natural acts. Not so, says the French historian Henri-Jean Martin. "They are the most complex inventions ever achieved by the human brain." And, he adds, "the most fundamental . . . since they gave man mental tools that made all the rest possible."

In China writing has never been of the alphabetic type. Instead, thousands of symbolic characters, or ideograms, are used. Each represents a word or concept.

The writing that developed in ancient Egypt is called hieroglyphic; in Mesopotamia, cuneiform. We know of this ancient writing through durable stone and clay inscriptions. But other materials also came into use in the ancient world—such as palm leaves and papyrus.

Among the Mayan people of Mexico and Central America, writing appeared in the first century B.C. The Mayans used hieroglyphics carved

A MAYAN RELIEF CARVING FOUND ON A STONE MONUMENT AT TIKAL IN NORTHERN GUATEMALA. IT IS AN EXAMPLE OF THE CIVILIZATION'S HIEROGLYPHIC SCRIPT.

in stone to record the passage of time and the influence of the gods on it. No one has yet found the key to their graphic system, so most of their inscriptions are still a mystery to us.

The Aztecs, who developed a great civilization in Mexico during the fourteenth century A.D., used ideograms and even some phonetic signs. They wrote on a paperlike material to record their laws, rules for the domestic economy, tax regulations, mythology, calendars, and rituals.

The Greek world, between 2000 and 1200 B.C., developed at least three types of writing in succession. The earliest was a script resembling hieroglyphics, probably developed for accounting and recordkeeping. The next system was quite different. It used eighty-five signs, many ideograms, and marks apparently representing numbers. The third system, from around 1450 to 1200 B.C., was long undeciphered. Then, after World War II, two British scholars figured out that "linear B," as it was called, was a syllabic writing system—using written characters to spell out a single sound—that recorded the earliest known Greek dialect, Mycenean. This writing was found on tablets on the island of Crete and on the Greek mainland in two places.

Other natural substances less durable than clay tablets were also often tried: wood, bark, and palm leaves. In Egypt a swamp plant that grew in clumps more than ten feet high along the banks of the Nile River was the source of papyrus. The Egyptians used papyrus not only to write on but to make sails, sandals, loincloths, and baskets. It was so much in demand that a thriving industry was built upon its cultivation and development.

For writing, sheets of papyrus were glued end to end to form a scroll. A medium-sized scroll would be some twenty sheets, each 16 by 16 inches (41 cm by 41 cm). One papyrus scroll now in the British Museum is 133 feet (41 m) long, 16 inches (41 cm) high, and contains 117 columns of writing. Professionals called scribes wrote on the scroll with a cut reed dipped in ink. Some of their documents on papyrus date back to 2500 B.C.

Papyrus was more convenient than clay tablets or stone slates. Papyrus would remain the material for correspondence, records—and books!—until well into the Christian era, when paper was invented in the Far East.

Scribes and Scrolls

It is hard to think of a scroll of parchment several feet long as a book. It doesn't look anything like the book you hold in your hands now. The word *book*, however, has come to have many meanings. It can refer to any quantity of sheets of paper or another material sewn or bound together. Now the primary meaning of the word is a written work either in manuscript or in printed form, and of any length, from a child's short picture book to a huge novel or academic study of a thousand pages or more.

Books weren't born until long after writing was widespread. Scribes in ancient Egypt began to extend their work beyond economic or religious matters. They created some books just for fun. Among their popular titles were *The Tale of the Eloquent Peasant* and *The Story of the Shipwrecked Sailor*, "published" on papyrus scrolls.

The ancient Greeks created a vast literature, written on large sheets of papyrus. Papyrus had reached Greece by the seventh century B.C., brought from Egypt by Greek mercenaries and merchants. The supply remained so small, however, that most Greeks kept writing on pottery fragments, waxed tablets, or bits of leather.

It was in Egypt that most of the examples of Greek writing on papyrus were discovered. This was the result of the conquest of Egypt in

A PORTION OF AN EGYPTIAN PAINTING ON A SCROLL OF PAPYRUS. IT IS A DETAIL FROM A BOOK CALLED *JUDGMENT OF THE DEAD*.

In a hall of the great library of Alexandria, Egypt, scholars converse while reading papyrus scrolls. Note the attendant taking a roll of parchment from a shelf.

332 B.C. by Alexander the Great, the young Macedonian. He made Egypt part of his empire, the largest the world had yet seen. To honor himself, he founded a city on Egypt's Mediterranean coast and named it Alexandria.

When Alexander died in 323 B.C., one of his Macedonian generals, Ptolemy I, took control of Egypt. He and his successors, called the Ptolemies, developed its economy, partly by massive exports of papyrus, and made the city of Alexandria a major center of Greek culture. Greek became the language of the ruling Greek and Macedonian elites. The Ptolemies stimulated science and scholarship using royal funds to build the Great Library and instructing scholars to gather Greek masterworks. Great numbers of scribes were put to work copying manuscripts for the Great Library. It is estimated that it held nearly half a million scrolls. For comparison, note that in the fourteenth century A.D., the largest library in Europe, at the Sorbonne (the University of Paris) in France, had about 1,700 books.

By the time of Cleopatra, the last of the Ptolemies, Alexandria was the greatest center of historical and scientific studies in the Western world. It is believed to have been the world's first true metropolis, a multicultural city with a population of about 600,000.

The Ptolemies were insatiable in their hunger for books. They ordered every ship passing through the port of Alexandria to hand over any manuscript or scroll on board for copying. The copy was then given to the visitors, while the Alexandrians kept the original. From the Athenians they got a set of the important Greek tragedies. And they paid a lot for what they believed to be the library of the philosopher Aristotle. Rulers around the world were called upon to send important books. The Ptolemies commissioned seventy-two Jewish scholars to translate the Torah, known now as the Septuagint, the ancient Greek Old Testament.

It is uncertain why so many treasures of the Great Library were lost, but one story has it that soldiers of the Roman emperor Aurelian (c. A.D. 212–275) burned the library during a war in the East. Some scholars believe that is a myth. There were several other major libraries in the ancient world, and the survival rate of their collections was little better than Alexandria's. In most such cases, what we have now are fragments, copies, or quotations in later texts. Manuscript experts suggest it was because ancient documents on papyrus were too perishable. Those that do survive almost intact, such as the famous Dead Sea Scrolls, were buried in dry caves or in a sealed container, like the tomb in the Nile Valley where one of the oldest-known Greek scrolls was found. Wars, fires, floods, political chaos—any of these might cause the loss and destruction of books.

Although ancient Rome is famous for the eloquence of its orators, writing and reading were common among its citizens. Historians find ample evidence of a literate population—posters, signs, plaques, countless graffiti on walls, records of civil life, even a familiarity with early Latin poets such as Ovid.

Even many slaves were trained to write. One of their chores was to copy books in Greek as well as in Latin. It was the author's original manuscript from which other direct copies were made. A specially trained slave, called the *librarius*, carried out this task and devised the page layout. He wrote on one side of the separate pages and then glued them together, end to end. A complex process, the result was a scroll, meant to be unrolled as the reader moved from one page to the next.

A revolution in the shape of the book began around the first century A.D. when scribes began to write on both sides of a page rather than on one side of a continuous scroll. The pages, cut up and sewn together in the shape we now know, greatly reduced the space needed for a book. A reader could hold it in one hand, and the compact size took up far less space in libraries. This new form was called a codex.

Letters have been found that tell us some writings were distributed in thousands of copies. Ancient Rome had bookstores that displayed new works on racks and promoted them with posters and flyers. Because of the empire's vast conquests, writers could boast that their works were being sold in the bookshops of provincial towns worldwide.

Still, the papyrus needed for book production was always scarce, and much had to be set aside for government records and business accounts. Shortages continued until a superior writing material—parchment—appeared.

According to Professor Martin, "parchment was made by taking the skins of sheep, goats or calves and first scraping them clean, removing the hairs, and rubbing them smooth with pumice. The skins were then washed, dressed with chalk, and the surfaces were finished with a lime-based wash."

Production of parchment rose rapidly when it was clear there was too little papyrus available. Its advantages were obvious: it resisted deterioration and would last indefinitely. It could also be produced in the West, so Europe need no longer worry about irregular shipments from the East. Animals were everywhere!

Yet there was one major drawback to parchment. It took an awful lot of skin to make just one book: two hundred animal skins in the case of one particular Bible. That meant parchment could be used only if the work was brief. Sometimes, to meet urgent demand, old parchments were washed and reused.

During the Middle Ages the abbeys and monasteries of Europe became centers for collecting and copying books. Manuscripts were acquired from pilgrims, and abbots had monks copy them. Both religious and secular texts were exchanged as cathedrals amassed extensive libraries.

In the twelfth century, book production in the monasteries ended as people began to supply the new universities with books. The universities supervised the copying of manuscripts, sending them out for commercial production by nonclerical copyists who worked for wages.

While the West was struggling with the problems of papyrus and parchment, as well as of supply and demand, far off in China a technological revolution was taking place that would make both those writing materials obsolete. The Chinese were finding out how to make paper, a far superior material. A process was initially developed around the

IN A THIRTEENTH-CENTURY EUROPEAN MONASTERY, MONKS ARE COPYING MANUSCRIPTS.

first century A.D. to make paper by reducing vegetable fibers to a pulp, placing it in molds or forms, and then drying it. The Chinese kept improving paper, for it proved to be a valuable commodity. Its use spread to Korea, Vietnam, and Japan, and reached into the Arab world. By the twelfth century, there were 400 paper mills in Morocco alone.

Paper to be used for writing became more available and of better quality as innovations in the making of paper multiplied. More and more paper mills sprang up in Europe. As paper became more widespread, literate people became their own scribes. With so much of the new writing material on hand, what would be the next step? To find a way to reproduce images and texts in multiple copies.

Printing . . .

THREE

Was China First?

After refining their papermaking techniques, the Chinese began to experiment with early methods of printing. The literature China created is enormous and grows with every generation. Some 15,000 manuscripts dated from the fifth to the tenth centuries have been found in China's walled-in caves. Among them were different forms of what we call a book. Texts of Chinese prayers were often engraved on stone slabs. Moistened paper was pressed onto the inscription stones, and when the paper was brushed with ink, the cut characters stood out white against the blackened paper.

The Chinese also developed the image engraved in relief and in reverse, a major step toward the printing of books. As the engravers'

IN THIS CHINESE SILK PAINTING, AN ARTISAN ON THE LEFT CUTS CHARACTERS INTO A PIECE OF WOOD. ON THE RIGHT, USING A BRUSH, A MAN SECURES AN IMPRESSION BY PRESSING A PIECE OF RICE PAPER AGAINST THE INKED WOODCUT.

skills improved, high-quality impressions were made on paper, too. Soon prayers were reproduced in this form as well as popular texts such as calendars and dictionaries.

Somewhat later, in the thirteenth century, printers in the great urban centers of China began producing booklets from woodcuts, well suited to their

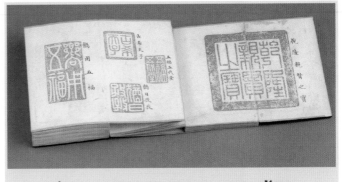

A SMALL BOOK OF SEAL IMPRINTS, MADE IN KOREA

ideographic writing system. The technique allowed for printing an image and its text together.

The thousands of signs in Chinese writing could be cut in blocks of soft wood. Each character was cut into a piece of wood in reverse by removing all the surrounding wood. These raised lines were dyed and rubbed on paper, producing a positive print of the desired text.

Very soon, movable characters came into use. In 1041, a blacksmith, Pi Cheng, made movable type of individual characters from a fire-hardened mixture of clay and liquid glue. His process was not wholly successful. Then Wang Tzhen had 60,000 individual wood characters cut, using them to publish about 100 copies of a local paper.

In the twelfth and thirteenth centuries both China and Korea printed works with metallic, movable type. Metallic type lasted much longer than wooden blocks, which wore out quickly. In 1403 a Korean ruler ordered the royal print shop to cast movable bronze characters in the hope of hastening the spread of new policies throughout his kingdom.

Although movable type became more and more widespread in its use, block printing was still cheaper and continued to be the common method. A wooden block carved with the image of the entire page was ultimately more economical to use than casting each letter or symbol individually. The huge number of ideographic characters in the Chinese language made letterpress printing very costly. (An alphabet of only twenty-six letters has a great advantage in that respect.)

Playing cards, using human and animal figures, probably made in Germany around 1450

Strangely, travelers to Asia never mentioned the use of printing there. Marco Polo, the Venetian who visited China in the thirteenth century, loved to examine and report on everything strange or new. He made note of banknotes he saw, but did not recognize that they had been printed from engraved blocks.

The technique of printing with movable type never caught on in China as it would in the West. Like other Chinese inventions, and there were many, it was dropped for a time and revived later.

Centuries would pass before Europe came to printing. In the West, wood sculptors learned to engrave wood blocks to print textiles. At first, repetitive designs were tried, then scenes. By the early 1400s Europeans were printing woodcuts on paper. A common subject was the playing card. A great many prints were of religious scenes or figures. Reading itself had taken hold long before. During the Middle Ages the rise of towns and commerce and the founding of the new universities increased demand for records, documents, and texts. Much of the writing would no longer be in the sacred tongue (Latin) but in the vernacular, the everyday speech of the nation or region. That opened the way to broader groups of readers.

The demand for books was so great that scribes could not keep up with it. Ingenious methods were devised to produce more reading material. Manuscripts were prepared and bound in separate sections so that scribes could divide the labor of copying, and several people could read the parts at the same time.

The labor of preparing manuscripts, copying them, and distributing them was immense. Surely someone would think of a better way to make books. That the Chinese already had, no one in Europe knew. Here was an ever-larger reading public, stimulated by the rise of universities. Professors needed texts, reference works, and commentaries on the classics. Guilds of scribes were organizing in each university town, and booksellers opened shops to serve the expanded reading class. In the thirteenth and fourteenth centuries, as many as 2,000 copies of such classic authors as Aristotle were produced. In the same period, books read simply for entertainment, or popular literature, appeared to satisfy the desires of a new merchant class as well as the long-established nobility and clergy.

A portrait of Francesco Petrarch (1304–1374), the Italian poet and humanist, made in the sixteenth century

Most writers could not live on the proceeds of their work, so they searched for rich patrons as the sure way to success. Those who found such support could live by their pens in exchange for some of their creative freedom.

Deluxe editions of books were created to suit elegant taste, with Europe's finest artists providing richly colored illuminations—adornment using brilliant colors and designs. Cheap editions were turned out, too, almost by methods of standardized mass production. The popular *Travels of Sir John Mandeville*, for example, created in manuscript form in 1356, appeared in German, Dutch, French, Latin, Spanish, Italian, Danish, Czech, and Irish translations, as well as in English.

The works of some of the ancient world's most influential figures were long thought to be lost. Two young Italians of the 1300s—Petrarch and Boccaccio—who became friends, searched relentlessly and found the missing writings of such men as Cicero, Ovid, and Tacitus. Petrarch, himself a great humanist, has been called the first modern man. His one insatiable desire, "which I have so far been unable to control," was for books. He couldn't get enough of them. "There is something special about books," he said. "[G]old and silver, jewels and purple raiment, marble halls and well-tended fields, pictures and horses in all their trappings, and everything else of that kind can afford only passing pleasure with nothing to say, whereas books can warm the heart with friendly words and counsel, entering into a close relationship with us which is articulate and alive."

Halfway into the next century, a great leap forward in the technology of book production would change everything—for readers, for writers, and for world culture.

A PORTRAIT OF JOHANN GUTENBERG, THE GERMAN PRINTER. NOTE THE SYMBOLIC TYPE MOLD IN HIS HAND.

FOUR

How Gutenberg Did It

Johann Gutenberg is the man given principal credit for inventing the new technology of printing. Although the Chinese and Koreans had long preceded him in the field, he knew nothing of their work. As with many inventions, numbers of creative minds often work independently of one another to provide solutions to a problem or to satisfy a need their society presents them.

Not much detail is known about Gutenberg's life. Born around the year 1400 in the German town of Mainz, he was the youngest son of a merchant. In the Middle Ages, Mainz was among the wealthiest cities along the Rhine River, presided over by an archbishop of great power. The Rhine was a primary route for trade throughout Europe, bringing prosperity to nearby craftsmen and merchants. The archbishop's court encouraged all branches of the arts and crafts.

Some scholars think the Gutenberg family was linked to a mint where gold coins were produced. That would mean mastering the technical skills used in working with metal. Johann was probably educated in one of the seminaries or convent schools of Mainz. Possibly he entered higher education at the nearby University of Erfurt.

Records indicate Gutenberg moved in and out of Mainz at various

Prelũ Ascẽsianũ

THIS TITLE PAGE FROM A BOOK PRINTED IN PARIS IN 1511 DEPICTS BOTH TYPESETTING AND THE PRINTING PRESS.

times in his youth. When both parents died he received a small inheritance. From a surviving letter we know that Gutenberg was living in Strasbourg in 1434, where he remained for the next eleven years. It too was a lively trading center. There he became a member of the goldsmith's guild, indicating he had mastered the craft of metalworking.

Gutenberg left Strasbourg in 1444, and there is no firm evidence of what he did for the next four years. He was back in Mainz in 1448, according to the record of a loan he received from his brother-in-law. That suggests he had already developed parts of his printing process and needed money to carry out his work. Some specimens of printing at Mainz from the year 1448 survive—a poem on the Last Judgment, Latin grammar books, and a calendar.

In 1450 Gutenberg convinced a wealthy man, Johann Fust of Mainz, to loan him the money needed to finance the completion of his invention and to print the so-called forty-two-line Bible. The collateral for the loan was the printing equipment to be built with this money. The work was carried out in the years 1453 to 1455.

During these years several thousand so-called letters of indulgence were turned out on Gutenberg's press, each dated and issued with the name of the buyer. Indulgences were the slips of paper offering written dispensation from sin that the Church sold to fund Crusades, new buildings, and other projects. As the handwritten versions grew obsolete, press runs of 200,000 indulgences at a time became common. It was a great source of income for the Church. And it showed how immensely profitable the invention of printing could be. All along, Gutenberg did his best to keep the details of his invention secret, for fear others might copy it and compete.

How did Gutenberg develop his invention? By combining several techniques already in use, including those of the screw press used for making wine and olive oil; the goldsmith's punch; an oil-based ink; impressionable paper; and the alphabetic scripts developed over thousands of years, which now lent themselves to printing with movable

AN ARTIST'S VERSION OF JOHANN GUTENBERG IN HIS WORKSHOP, EXAMINING HIS FIRST PROOF SHEET

type. "New technologies and materials," the historian Jared Diamond has demonstrated, "make it possible to generate still other new technologies by recombination." Gutenberg's most important innovation was the molding and casting of movable metal type. It was the first application of the theory of interchangeable parts, a basic principle of the machine age yet to come.

Gutenberg carved each letter of the alphabet onto the end of a steel punch, and hammered it into a copper blank. He then took the copper impression, inserted it into a mold, and poured a molten alloy of lead, antimony, and bismuth (all metals) into it. The alloy cooled quickly, leaving a reverse image of the letter attached to a lead base. The width of the lead base varied according to the size of the letter. An *I* for instance, would not take up as much space as a *w*.

The type was pressed onto the paper. The result? A printed page with such a perfect regularity it seemed magical to the first viewers. The masterwork forever linked to Gutenberg's name is the Bible, each page forty-two lines long, published in two volumes. The first run was 300 copies, each volume selling for thirty florins. That was three years of a clerk's wages.

Probably. Maybe. Likely—these words often occur in the description of the development of printing. It means documentary evidence is scarce. Scholars searching the archives find little material. And the evidence that has survived is often hard to interpret. Then too, when a new technique has just been born, its creators often don't have the vocabulary to describe the tools and materials they were working with. Local historians only hint, at times, of what was going on in the neighborhood. So we can only do our best, with limited means, to figure out what really happened, who did what, and what the meaning of it is.

The new technique greatly reduced the cost of manufacturing a book. It could reproduce several hundred identical copies of any text. In Gutenberg's time the average print run was about 500 copies.

Successful and beautiful as these first products of his invention were, Gutenberg somehow defaulted on his loan. Gutenberg lost his printing workshop when a court order forced him to turn over the machinery and type to Fust.

In addition to the type designed for the Bible, Gutenberg had to give over the copious stock of type prepared for an edition of the Psalter, a collection of hymns from the Hebrew Bible. This was printed in 1457 by Fust with Gutenberg's former apprentice, Schoeffer, as his partner. It included new type in two sizes as well as beautiful initial letters set off by the addition of a second color.

It must have been a horrible blow to the inventor to lose all this. Somehow he got himself going again and created a new printing operation

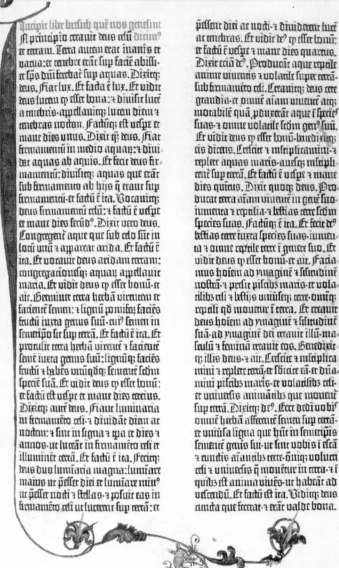

A PAGE FROM THE GUTENBERG BIBLE, PRINTED IN MAINZ, GERMANY

with financial assistance from a wealthy lawyer. Several small items such as medical calendars, leaflets, and inventories were produced with a set of small types he fashioned like the round cursive handwriting used in many manuscript books at that time.

Not much more is known about Gutenberg. His last years were spent in the court of an archbishop of Nassau. His appointment carried with it an allowance for clothing and other necessities. He died on February 3, 1468, and was buried in a churchyard that no longer exists. His native city of Mainz now has two monuments erected to his memory, and a museum, which includes a recreation of his press and workshop.

Gutenberg's most enduring memorial, however, is the printing that would reach into every corner of the world.

Several print shops were soon operating in Mainz itself, producing many books on a commercial scale. As printing became more efficient, masters learned to combine letterpress with illustrations engraved in wood. Pupils of the early printers began spreading across Europe, teaching others how to use printing to extend the spread of information and ideas.

Isabella

Saluatorie

Conceptois

ma rie

A CRUDE WOODCUT PRINTED WITH THE "COLUMBUS LETTER" OF 1493 SHOWS ISLANDS THE EXPLORER VISITED IN THE WEST INDIES. IN THE FOREGROUND IS A SPANISH SHIP WITH COLUMBUS ON DECK.

Printing, Printing, Everywhere

In 1462 Gutenberg's hometown underwent a catastrophe. The troops of Adolf of Nassau conquered Mainz and great numbers of citizens fled to safety—printers among them. The printers were welcomed wherever they went. Research has brought up the names of more than a thousand of them, mostly of German origin, who ran workshops in fifteenth-century Europe. In Italy more than one hundred printers have been recorded, thirty in France, twenty-six in Spain, five in Switzerland, two in Bohemia, eight in Holland, five in Belgium, one in Poland, and four in England. All told, by 1480 printing presses were operating in more than 110 towns in Europe.

That century, the fifteenth, marks the transition from the Middle Ages to modern times. Wherever you dip into its history, you find far-reaching changes taking place. Recall that this was the time when Columbus and other European navigators opened up new worlds. (The "Columbus Letter," which he wrote to announce his first Atlantic crossing, was printed in Basel, Switzerland, in 1493.) The city of Florence under the Medici, the powerful family that ruled Florence from the fifteenth to the eighteenth centuries, became the center of Renaissance culture. It was the era of great artists such as Leonardo da Vinci, Michelangelo, and Dürer. In the early sixteenth century, the astronomer

THE ENGLISH PRINTER WILLIAM CAXTON EXAMINES A PROOF SHEET IN A SUMPTUOUS WORKSHOP WHILE A WOMAN CARRIES IN REFRESHMENTS.

Copernicus made his mark. But not all was positive. This was also the time of the Inquisition, when thousands were tortured, burned, or exiled because of their beliefs, and many long-lasting wars for power took untold numbers of lives. Slavery, which had started a long time before in the early history of humankind, began to expand enormously when in 1442 a Portuguese ship captured blacks on the coast of Africa and thus began the European slave trade.

In printing, the first primitive presses were gradually being refined. For the next 300 years—between the fifteenth and eighteenth centuries—shops would print at an astonishing speed.

Printing was a major influence on the formation of a standard language in England. The first English printer was William Caxton (about 1421–1491). Born in Kent, he served an apprenticeship in the cloth trade, then went to Brugge, Belgium, where he headed an English trading company. In 1469 he translated into English a French account of the Trojan Wars. Then he moved on to Cologne in Germany where he spent eighteen months learning the trade of printing. Back in Brugge, he set up a press, and published the first book to be printed in English—his translation of the Trojan War story. In 1476 Caxton returned to England and placed his wooden press in a shop within the precincts of Westminster Abbey. A year later he published the first dated book to be printed in England.

Caxton published around one hundred items, several in more than one edition. Included were two editions of Chaucer's *Canterbury Tales*, the *Fables of Aesop*, and several books with chivalry as their theme. He translated from French, Latin, and Dutch, sometimes adding his own foreword or afterword. One of his typefaces is the original Old English type. Experts rate him a superb craftsman, perhaps the finest printer of his day.

From the time of Chaucer in the 1300s to about 1800, the English language continued to change in several ways. Printing itself, scholars think, was a key factor in the evolution of the language. It fostered norms of spelling and punctuation and gave people many more opportunities to write and to reach a much wider audience for their work.

There was as yet no uniform language in England. The regional dialects varied so much that many people couldn't make themselves understood when trying to talk with others in their own country. As an editor of manuscripts submitted to him, and as their printer, Caxton earned much credit for standardizing the language.

Though a businessman and not a scholar, Caxton had to make decisions on several issues, says David Crystal, a linguistics expert:

- Should he use foreign words in his translation or replace them with native English words?

- Which variety of English should he follow, given the existence of major regional differences?

- Which literary style should he use as a model? Chaucerian English? Or something less "ornate"?

- How should the language be spelled and punctuated, given the scribal variations of the previous centuries?

- In publishing native writers, should he change their language to make it more widely understood?

The tale of the chanons yeman

¶ And begynneth the tale

Ith this chanon I duellyd vij yere
And of his saience am I neuer the new
Al that I had I haue loft ther by
And god woot so haue mo than I
There as I was wont to be right freffh & gay
Of clothynge and of other good aray
Now may I were an hofe vp on myn hed
And where my colour was both freffh & rede
Now it is wan and of a ledyn helve
Who so it vfith fore fhal he relve
And of my fwynk y blent is myn eye
Lo fucke auauntage it is to multeplye
That flydyng faience hath made me fo bare
That I haue no good where that euer I fare
And yet I am endettid fo fore therby
Of gold that I borowed treblly

A PAGE FROM WILLIAM CAXTON'S EDITION OF GEOFFREY CHAUCER'S
THE CANTERBURY TALES, AROUND 1484

These were tough practical problems. To achieve a decent sale, a book had to be understood throughout England. Yet could you satisfy everyone at a time when the language was very much in flux? Caxton once complained that even the simple word *egg* wasn't universally understood. And punctuation? That remains an issue to this day.

At the close of the fifteenth century, only fifty years after Gutenberg's invention, about 15 million copies had been printed in Europe. The book trade did best in university towns and large commercial centers. But it also became a big international business, controlled by wealthy investors.

The clergy quickly saw the advantage of the printing press, not only for indulgences but theological texts and even manuals on how to conduct inquisitions. But it proved harder to control what printers issued than what secular scribes had done.

Martin Luther (1483–1546), the German priest who launched the Protestant Reformation in 1517, found wide readership when printed texts of his theses were rapidly distributed.

Greater freedom promoted far-reaching discussions that led to mounting opposition to the Catholic Church's established role as the sole custodian of spiritual truth. Bibles were printed in vernacular languages rather than in Latin. Now people could read scriptures for themselves, said the Lutherans. Since

Where did the typefaces we are familiar with come from?

They are either imitations of early handwritten letters or were modeled after the lettering in manuscript books. The standard roman capital and lowercase letters were adapted by Nicolas Jenson, a Frenchman who learned printing in Germany and set up shop in Venice. The manuscript books of Venetian monks were his models. His beautiful typeface has not been significantly improved upon.

Practically all roman typefaces in common use now have accompanying italics, first used in 1501 by Aldus Manutius, the Venetian printer, for an edition of the poet Virgil.

William Caslon, born in 1692, in Worcestershire, changed the look of English printing with his design and casting of a new typeface named after him. His style is followed by many typographers of today. William Baskerville, another English printer, born in 1706, designed types that are halfway between the old-style roman of Caslon and the modern roman letter created by the Italian printer Bodoni.

PORTRAIT OF MARTIN LUTHER

there was no need for the Church to interpret it, a person's relationship with God could be more direct and personal.

As religious dissension mounted, the Catholic Counter-Reformation encouraged an expansion of the Catholic press. The Jesuits founded colleges throughout Europe and invited printers to work alongside them. New monasteries and convents founded in Catholic Europe included libraries and welcomed a new religious literature.

A network of Protestant presses faced off against a network of Catholic presses. Secular literature also kept expanding as printing firms multiplied. The Elzevier press in Holland, for instance, printed large editions of classical authors and pirated the works of leading English and French authors. The pirated editions were meant for a public ignorant of Latin and hungry for books in their own language.

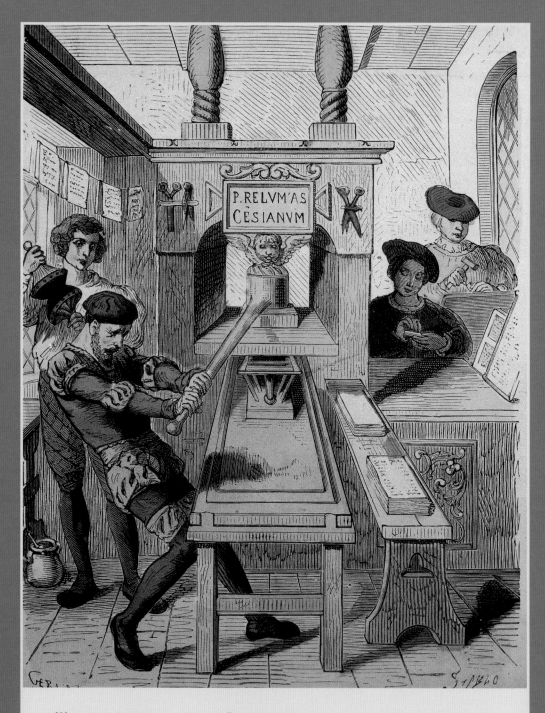

WORKMEN OPERATING A PRESS IN A PARISIAN PRINT SHOP OF THE SIXTEENTH CENTURY

The Print Shop: A Cultural Center

The early printers were businessmen, of course, out to make a profit from the new invention. But they played other roles, too. They served the arts and sciences as well. By promoting work in many such fields, they indirectly encouraged culture. Their workshops were different from other manufacturing operations because they became gathering places for scholars, artists, and writers, as well as sanctuaries for foreign translators, émigrés, and refugees. Here there was room for every kind of cultural interchange. Print shops added a new element to urban life almost everywhere.

This was an enterprise that the women of Europe participated in, as well as men. The daughters and widows of printers often took over the family workshop. Nuns also did religious printing. In the convent of San Jacopo di Ripoli the nuns who ran its press published a notable Italian translation of Plato's *Dialogues* in an edition of more than a thousand copies.

In time, the business of printing greatly expanded. Printers distributed handbills, circulars, and sales catalogs, and peddled their books wherever a market existed.

To get their own names before the public, early printers put their

ILLUSTRATION FROM AN ITALIAN COOKBOOK OF THE 1580S, ONE OF THE MANY POPULAR
HOW-TO MANUALS OF THAT ERA

firm's name and shop address on the title pages of their books. Of course they also promoted the authors and artists whose work they printed, building their celebrity through advertising.

Job printing went along with book printing. Printers sought all sorts of odd assignments to increase profits: not only commercial advertising, but the official propaganda of the court and the counter-propaganda of rebels. The printing of tons of government documents was just as common then as it is now.

How-to manuals were another source of printing revenue. The subjects included cooking, proper behavior for young ladies, etiquette for social climbers, accounting methods for aspiring businessmen, medical advice for the sick, craft manuals for apprentices. . . . Whatever anyone wanted or needed, a printer was ready to publish.

An invaluable aspect of early printing was what it did for illustrations. Printers mastered the image just as they had the word. Many caricatures and cartoons were published. Bibles, whether for Protestants or Catholics, included illustrations. The great northern artists—Dürer, Cranach, and Holbein—owed much to print. The new arts of printing and engraving increased the exposure of their work and helped to launch art history.

This was a time that also saw the birth of an entirely new form of printed literature—the picture book, meant to teach children how to behave.

In certain fields of learning—geometry, geography, anatomy, architecture—the image linked to the text acted as "a savior for Western science," wrote the historian George Sarton. Figures, maps, charts, and diagrams were indispensable aids to memory, as well as paths to richer understanding of difficult material.

The greatest print shop of the sixteenth century was run by Christopher Plantin in Antwerp, Belgium. It contained 22 presses, 160 workmen, and numerous fonts for different languages and formats. His was a vast publishing empire, built by his ability to win rich and powerful friends in different regions. He secured the backing of Spain's King Philip II (1527–1598), who appointed him to supervise the printing industry throughout the Low Countries (part of Spain's empire). At the same time Plantin was working for Calvinists, who opposed the religious climate of the Low Countries. He was the kind of businessman whose views were not rigid, enabling him to survive and prosper even in times of religious warfare. Such enterprising publishers were simply more interested in profit than politics.

Aldus Manutius, a Roman scholar and teacher, was another famous printer. Around 1490 he set up a shop in Venice financed by a prince of Capri whose sons he had tutored. He began printing ancient Greek classics available only in manuscript before then. By 1515, when he died, his Aldine Press had printed twenty-seven editions of important Greek authors as well as numerous works of reference. He also published books in Latin, Italian, and Hebrew. His press is also known for producing the first italic type, modeled on the handwriting of Petrarch. His shop housed a staff of scholarly proof correctors, illustrators, and translators. He had occasional visitors as well, there to see what was going on, or to recite a poem or a piece of prose to Aldus in the hope that he would publish it for them. When Aldus died, his son Paulus took over the Aldine Press.

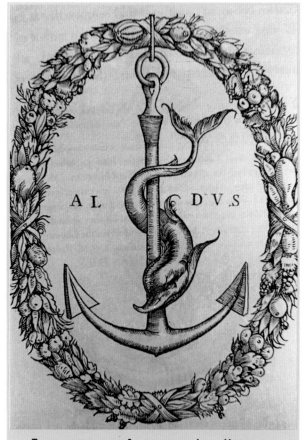

THE TRADEMARK OF THE ITALIAN PRINTER ALDUS MANUTIUS, DISPLAYING HIS CHARACTERISTIC DOLPHIN-AND-ANCHOR DESIGN

A PORTRAIT OF THE DUTCH HUMANIST ERASMUS BY QUENTIN METSYS

A major effect of printing was to widen the career opportunities of intellectuals. Some became scholar-printers, like Manutius. Others worked for printers, correcting proofs, making indexes, translating, or writing new books on commission from printer-publishers. Erasmus (c. 1466–1536) of Rotterdam, the most eminent European scholar of his time, did so well with the books he wrote that he didn't need to depend on patrons, a rare achievement. All too many authors, like Cervantes, good as they were, died poor. Printing itself led more men and women to write. With printed books available, writers were inspired by imaginative work they might not otherwise have seen. The desire to express yourself in a personal literary form and to have it read by a wider audience than ever before was encouraged by the progress of printing.

In Venice, Paris, London, and other cities in the late sixteenth century, writers produced such publications as chronologies (timelines or tables of important historical dates), cosmographies (descriptions of the known universe), dictionaries, and other guides to knowledge. An increasing number of writers and scholars were supporting themselves through a combination of publishing and patronage. If you knew your way around the court and made friends with the right people, you could build a career in literature. The French playwright Racine and the poet Boileau received generous pensions from Louis XIV.

In sixteenth-century England, Queen Elizabeth I was a generous patron of the theater. She supported her own Players Company and often selected Shakespeare's plays for court performances. Shakespeare also enjoyed the patronage of the Earl of Southampton. Shakespeare's plays did so well at the box office, however, that he became quite prosperous before he retired.

Take a look at the excerpt on page 55 that is from the earliest printed edition of Shakespeare's plays. Though it may look difficult at first glance, try reading it yourself for fun. You'll see how spelling and punctuation varied from what you are used to now.

The Bard Gets Published

The earliest printed edition of all of William Shakespeare's plays did not appear until 1623, seven years after his death. The title page of the volume reads: "The Workes of William Shakespeare, containing all his Comedies, Histories and Tragedies. Truly set forth, according to the first Originall." In the front of the edition, the two editors, the actors John Heminge and Henry Condell, included this message "To the Great Variety of Readers."

From the most able, to him that can but spell: There you are number'd. We had rather you were weighd. Especially when the fate of all Bookes depends vpon your capacities: and not of your heads alone, but of your purses. Well! It is now publique, & you will stand for your priuiledges wee know: to read, and censure. Do so, but buy it first. That doth best commend a Booke, the Stationer saies. Then, how odde soeuer your braines be, or your wisedomes, make your licence the same, and spare not. Judge your sixe-pen'orth, your shillings worth, your fiue shwillings worth at a time, or higher, so you rise to the iust rates, and welcome. But, what euer you do, Buy. Censure will not driue a Trade, or make Iacke go. And though you be a Magistrate of wit, and sit on the Stage at Blacke-Friers, or the Cock-pit, to arraigne Playes dailie, know, these Playes haue had their triall alreadie, and stood out all Appeales; and do now come forth quitted rather by a Decree of Court, then any purchas'd Letters of commendation.

It had bene a thing, we confesse, worthie to haue bene wished, that the Author himselfe had liu'd to haue set forth, and ouerseen his owne writings; But since it hath bin ordain'd otherwise, and he by death departed from that right, we pray you do not envie his Friends, the office of their care, and paine, to haue collected & publish'd them; and so to haue publish'd them, as where (before) you were abus'd with diuerse stolne, and surreptitious copies, maimed, and deformed by the frauds and stealthes of iniurious imposters, that expos'd them; euen those, are now offer'd to your view cur'd, and perfect of their limbes; and all the rest, absolute in their numbers, as he conceiued them. . .

John Heminge
Henrie Condell

THE TITLE PAGE OF THE FIRST FOLIO OF SHAKESPEARE'S PLAYS

The edition includes the names of all the principal actors in Shakespeare's company. Probably about 1,000 copies were printed as the joint venture of four men. About one-fourth of that edition, having escaped disintegration and loss, is still around. The book sold for £1, a high price for the time. Not long ago a copy of that First Folio edition sold for a little more than $2 million.

AN AMUSING COPPER ENGRAVING MADE IN FRANCE IN THE LATE 1600S PORTRAYS THE ITINERANT
PRINTER WHO WAS REPORTER, TYPESETTER, AND INDEPENDENT BUSINESSMAN ALL IN ONE. HE WAS
OFTEN SEEN AT FAIRS OFFERING "CURIOUS NEWS" OF SUCH EVENTS AS THE BIRTH OF QUINTUPLETS,
THE LAUNCHING OF WARS, OR THE SIGHTING OF COMETS.

From Apprentice to Master

Within a few years after Gutenberg's invention, print shops began to take on the features of modern manufacturing. Techniques were perfected to achieve standardized production. Journeymen printers were expected to finish a task in a specified time. Though they worked with their hands, they lived with books, knew authors and scholars, and mingled in the world of ideas.

Journeymen entered the trade as apprentices. You could be anywhere from twelve to twenty-one years of age when starting out. Few or no girls became apprentices, though some did become printers. It didn't matter whether your father was a locksmith, cobbler, carpenter, weaver, wine merchant, apothecary, bailiff, soldier, or, of course, printer. You had to be able to read and write and know some Latin. The period of apprenticeship ran from two to five years. The master was obliged to teach you the craft, to board and house you, to keep you in clothes, and to allow you some pocket money.

An apprenticeship was hardly fun. You were the servant of the journeyman. You got out of bed very early to neaten up the workshop, light the fire in winter, and set the table. You prepared the ink and dampened the sheets before printing. You helped on the press, an exhausting job, and if you wanted to become a compositor, you set type under the watchful eye of an expert supervisor.

A SCENE FROM ONE OF THE LARGER PRINT SHOPS OF THE SEVENTEENTH CENTURY

You ran errands outside, too, such as delivering proofs or picking them up. And when the day's work had ended for everyone else, and they'd all gone home, you had to put everything in order before heading to bed.

Upon finishing your apprenticeship, you became a journeyman—still young, free to do what you wished, and a bachelor, since apprentices were not allowed to marry. Off you went on your journeys, moving from town to town, taken on by printers here and there, for a month, a year, or maybe more. Once you were a journeyman, you were free to marry. If you married the master's daughter or his widow—a big step up the ladder—you could settle down in his town. If not, picking up more skill and experience, you were likely to finally settle down in whatever place was prime for opening a print shop of your own.

Most print shops in the early centuries were small. A master printer usually had two presses; the largest might have six. Expenses were high—for equipment, paper, type, and wages. The masters had to rely on rich merchants for capital investment. It was hard to make a living and a profit. The only way was to increase working hours and reduce wages.

Master printers usually fed their workers in their homes—living quarters were attached to the shop. But to save money they might force the workers to eat at their own expense in the taverns. Or master printers might take on extra apprentices to handle the press. These extra workers were not paid but simply gained experience. In the big shops the working day was longer than in many other trades: perhaps twelve hours, from 5:00 A.M. to 7:00 P.M., with a high output demanded of everyone. Despite the heavy workload, printers were not paid better than other workers. Usually very poor, they lived in one room with their family.

No wonder some workers protested, demanding better conditions and higher wages. They formed brotherhoods (the forerunners of trade unions). If their demands weren't met, sometimes they went on strike. This happened as early as 1502. The French city of Lyons, which had about one hundred presses, with a total workforce of about a thousand—apprentices, compositors, pressmen, proofreaders, and master printers—was the site of a big strike in 1539. The strikers took to the streets, inventing a grotesque creature—the Printer's Devil—whom they saluted as they passed. Another such strike broke out in 1572. Both strikes failed. Labor wars in the printing trade are recorded in Paris, Geneva, and Venice (in Aldus Manutius's print shop).

It would shock any author of today to learn how free compositors

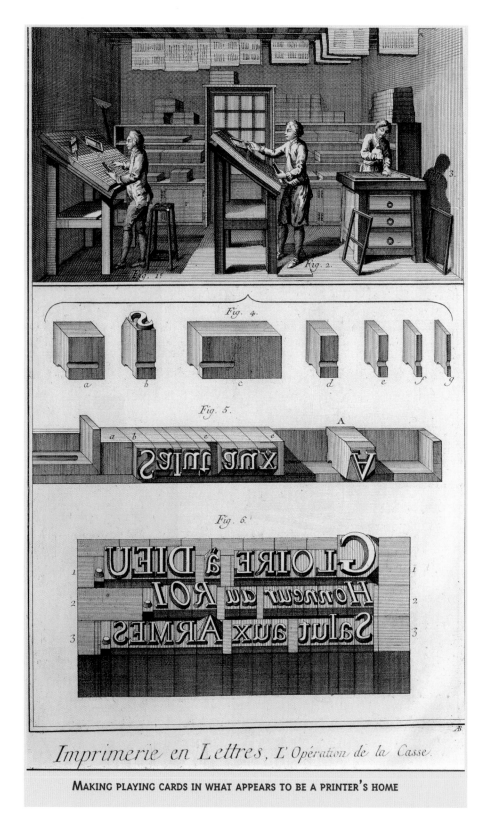

Imprimerie en Lettres, L'Opération de la Casse.

MAKING PLAYING CARDS IN WHAT APPEARS TO BE A PRINTER'S HOME

in the 1600s were to rewrite manuscripts. The compositor, who set the type for the book, was expected to be highly skilled and to work very rapidly. The task required the swift coordination of manual dexterity, memory, and aesthetic judgment. The historian Adrian Johns notes that "a compositor did not just slavishly copy a writer's manuscript. On the contrary, he enjoyed substantial freedom in his settings." A master printer like the Londoner Joseph Moxson had a reputation to maintain, and his compositor was called upon to re-work the author's text so as to remove any "careless" or "ignorant" faults. He was even asked to get into the meaning of the author and to "use typography to make that meaning clearer than any author could."

Printing presses multiplied between the fifteenth and eighteenth centuries. And so did the number of books produced. Except for the textbooks the increasing number of schools and colleges required, most books interested only a small number of readers. While an almost infinite number of identical copies could be produced once the type was set, the problem was to reduce the cost of each copy by printing as many as possible. It was foolish, however, to print more copies of a title than the market could absorb in a reasonable amount of time.

By 1600 a big press run for a book was around 1,500 copies. Most editions of major works varied between 1,000 and 2,000. In the eighteenth century printings were still usually under 2,000. A major exception was Diderot's great *Encyclopedia*. Its press run was 4,250 copies. Remember that in those times the population of towns was much smaller, transport by boat or wagon very difficult, and some printers pirated books.

Books went out of print much more slowly than now. A secondhand or used-book market flourished early on. Dealers stocked up by bidding for books of scholars when they died. And then there were the hordes of street peddlers, who sold everything from simple alphabet

THIS 1751 ENGRAVING OF WOMEN WORKING IN A PAPER FACTORY IS ONE OF THE GREAT NUMBER OF CRAFTS ILLUSTRATED IN DIDEROT'S *ENCYCLOPEDIA*.

books to almanacs, calendars, romances, and Catholic and Protestant pamphlets. Banned books, too, were the more desirable because forbidden.

The first broadsheets—long pieces of paper containing several pages of a work printed on one side only—were peddled on the street, along with roughly drawn prints. It was a popular culture reaching out to the uneducated and barely literate and to the many who wanted books that couldn't be sold openly in the bookshops.

The international book trade kept growing, centered in cities such as Lyons and Frankfurt. They ran book fairs annually. Dealers from many European nations flowed in and out, with ordinary readers buying, too. Despite the international character of the business, there was no agreement on publishing rights. Any legislation was local and incomplete. Pirated editions were common. So was censorship, exercised by all sorts of authorities. Where copyright protection did exist, it was only local or national, and other printer-publishers beyond that realm could counterfeit an edition at much lower cost and sell it at a nice profit.

Pub July 4th 1795 by H. Humphrey N. 37
New Bond Street

THIS FANCIFUL PAINTING OF SIR JOSEPH BANKS WAS DONE BY ENGLISH ARTIST JAMES GILLRAY (1757–1815). IT HIGHLIGHTS HIS LIFE AS AN EXPLORER AND A NATURALIST.

An Aid to Science

The impact of the printing press on science was immense. Printing was used to report and maintain knowledge about the world of nature. It made scientific studies more readily available, spreading knowledge to far wider circles than had ever been reached before printing. The early modern scientists used a variety of printed materials—books, periodicals, papers, letters, maps, graphs, and diagrams.

In the early stages of printing, the biological sciences especially were advanced as the dissemination of identical illustrations became possible. Think of anatomy, zoology, and botany, and imagine how enormously helpful accurate and standard illustrations must have been to researchers.

The new printed books aided the standardization of technical terms. Before Gutenberg, when manuscripts were copied by scribes, illustrations that had been beautifully done originally lost their detail over the course of centuries of hand copying. After Gutenberg, often with the help of some of the best artists, books of great technical accuracy and beauty flowed from the presses and increased the popularity of science.

Sir Joseph Banks, the British naturalist who sailed with Captain James Cook around the world, said that the engravings of the plants they observed, made upon his return, spoke "universally to all mankind."

An Italian artist's version of the Solar System based on the theories of Nicolaus Copernicus. The early-sixteenth-century Polish astronomer placed the Sun at the center of the Solar System with the planets revolving around it.

The readiness of printers to issue new books encouraged scientists to publish their discoveries. Thus new ideas were not lost, but reached the minds of others and brought progress. Not every scientist was eager to broadcast his findings. Some, such as Copernicus and da Vinci, withheld their work from the press for years. But such reluctance became more and more rare.

Scientists depended on the use of printed materials in the effort to create agreement on their pioneering work. Publication would stimulate contributions from other qualified researchers who would check observations, repeat experiments, create new tests, and offer fresh data. But issues of credibility often confused the picture because unauthorized reports were sometimes sneaked out and published even before a scientist could release his report. This happened often enough to create doubt in the scientific community. Plagiarism, and the distortion and errors typical of it, were all too common. Questions of bias in judgment came up, and reputations were tarnished. No wonder some scientists tried to keep their new discoveries secret, confiding them only to friends.

In that great age of exploration and discovery, the printed reports of the seafarers stimulated major advances in geography and in astronomical methods of navigation. Sea charts and land maps were printed in an attempt to represent pictorially the whole spherical surface of the Earth. Ptolemy's *Geography*, a classical survey of all Greek knowledge on the subject up to the second century A.D., unknown to the West for centuries, was translated into Latin. After its first printing in 1475, no fewer than seven editions were printed in the next quarter century.

That was an example of how the printed word wove a cultural web around western Europe. Printers began to engrave type characters so that they could publish works written in languages other than their own—English, French, Italian, Spanish, and even Hebrew. When Spain and then Portugal banished Jews faithful to their religion, several Jewish printers found refuge in Italy. One great publishing house in Venice—Daniel Bomberg's—printed the Babylonian Talmud and the

IN EARLY-EIGHTEENTH-CENTURY RUSSIA, CZAR PETER THE GREAT FOUNDED A PRINTING PRESS IN HIS GOVERNMENT OFFICES AND OPENED THE WAY TO A WIDER DISSEMINATION OF KNOWLEDGE.

Jerusalem Talmud. Soon there were Jewish printers in Constantinople, Prague, Kraków, Salonika, Morocco, Cairo, and Galilee.

In 1563 Czar Ivan the Terrible founded a Cyrillic print shop in Moscow. Russian printers issued hundreds of titles, but under the control of the religious authorities. It was Czar Peter the Great who liberated the modern Slavic book by founding a printing office in 1711 in his new capital, St. Petersburg. It broke with the past by publishing scientific books in Russian.

Later, in 1783, Catherine the Great freed printing from state control, and printers began to operate throughout Russia. But not for long! When the French Revolution exploded in 1789, Catherine, scared by revolutionary ferment, ended her liberal policy, closed all private printing firms, and opened censorship offices. The Russian upper class, however, continued to read foreign works in French or German.

Although China had been the first to create a form of movable type, not until the sixteenth century did a genuine printing industry develop there. For the nonalphabetic character of the Chinese language, woodcuts were better suited to mechanical duplication. Wood engraving was easy and cheap.

Both learned and popular works in Chinese were printed on presses and reached wide audiences through regional booksellers. The output included poetry, short stories, tales of the imperial family, word games, almanacs, encyclopedias, letter-writing manuals, even comic strips in color. By the end of the nineteenth century, it is estimated that between 30 and 45 percent of the males in China were literate. (Records for the number of literate females were not kept at the time.)

When Christian missionaries were allowed into Japan in the late 1500s, the Jesuits established presses in a few cities. They published first in Latin and then in Japanese written in the Latin alphabet. A century later, as the literacy rate in Japan rose to the level of Europe's, thousands of titles in Japanese were available to readers.

The Making of Maps

Where do you live?

No doubt you can name the street, the town, the state, and the nation. And if you paid attention in geography class, you have a pretty good idea of the world beyond your home.

It wasn't always like that.

Europeans of the Middle Ages had little knowledge of the world beyond their borders. Villagers often had no idea of the people or land a hundred miles away. It took many centuries before the wide spaces of the globe—the lands and the seas—were explored, and maps drawn to reveal those discoveries.

Maps represent spatial objects on a flat surface. Cartography, or mapmaking, is older than the art of writing. The ancient Babylonians, Egyptians, and Chinese drew maps. The oldest surviving map is on a Babylonian clay tablet dating around 2500 B.C. The ancient Greeks worked out the best system of cartography, and no one equaled it until the 1500s.

Knowledge of geography was slow to accumulate. It wasn't until the advent of the printing press that it reached more than a tiny minority. Printing increased the flow of the vast amount of information acquired from the voyagers of the early modern period. In the age of exploration and empire, the need for more knowledge opened the new universities to geography as a scholarly discipline.

Mapmaking became a tool of government. It was used to establish boundaries and to defend the state against its enemies. Philip II assigned a scholar to map the Iberian Peninsula, and Portugal had a scientist spend five years mapping the king's territories in the New World.

In France, in the 1600s, maps were made of each province, with the cartographers urged to greater accuracy. When contending powers came to an agreement over disputed territory, maps were made to avoid future disputes over what had been agreed upon. Peter the Great commissioned a German geographer to map his vast Russia. Early in the 1700s Britain had its colonies around the world surveyed, one by one, and only after that was done was England itself mapped.

Knowledge of the best trade routes was of great commercial value. Private companies took orders from the state to print maps of trade routes as well as of whole countries such as India. Maps and accounts of voyages became a valued part of printing catalogs. Geographic reference books multiplied after 1500. To

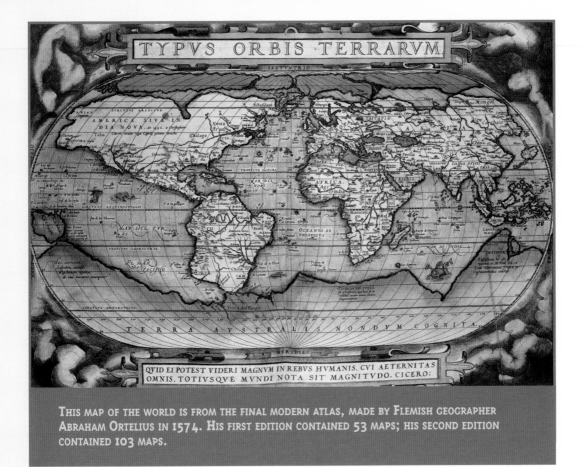

simplify the problem of finding the location of cities and regions, three of Europe's leading printers—Abraham Ortelius, Gerardus Mercator, and Willem Blaue—specialized in atlases.

Much later, in 1815, a map was printed "that changed the world," or our understanding of it. It was the work of William Smith (1769–1839), an English surveyor. After some twenty years of closely examining fossil-bearing sedimentary rock layers throughout Britain, he created the first geological map of the land. On a scale of 5 miles to the inch, the map, when put together on a wall, was 8-1/2 feet (2.6 m) high and 6 feet (1.8 m) across. It made an enormous contribution to the way people thought about Earth and its physical and biological evolution. Smith demonstrated that the study of fossils helps explain the history and development of the planet.

In the twentieth century the art and science of mapmaking were greatly advanced. Modern mapmakers used remote sensing by airplane and satellite radar, as well as hi-tech scanners, to collect and update data. Today maps of the world are available on a uniform scale.

An edition of a Lutheran Bible from around 1530 shows Babylon burning, an illustration of a passage from Revelation, Chapter 18.

From Luther to Plymouth Rock

The printing press had much to do with the spread of religious ideas. Scholars hold that Lutheranism was the child of the printed book. Between 1517 and 1520 Martin Luther issued thirty publications that sold about 300,000 copies, an immense circulation for that time, or even now. Through printing, Luther was able to make a powerful impression upon the minds of Europe. "For the first time in human history," according to Professor Elizabeth Eisenstein, "a great reading public judged the validity of revolutionary ideas through a mass medium which used the vernacular language together with the arts of the journalist and the cartoonist."

Luther was aware of the power of the new invention. He had already edited texts in Latin and German for printers and recognized how appealing their own language was to the public. It was as though by a stroke of magic that he found himself with his new ideas reaching out to the whole world. His followers also pioneered the use of cartoons and caricatures to reach a mass audience.

PILGRIMS SIGN THE MAYFLOWER COMPACT BEFORE LANDING IN 1620 TO FOUND THE PLYMOUTH COLONY, THE FIRST AMERICAN SETTLEMENT BASED ON A SOCIAL CONTRACT.

Dissent, religious or political, was not new. But when implemented by print, it could make a far deeper and broader impression than ever before. When Henry VIII of England broke with the Pope and created the Anglican Church, his government became the first state in Europe to mount a propaganda campaign through the press to solidify support.

The sixteenth-century schism within Christendom created a great many splinter groups, separatists, and independent sects. The lines of cleavage extended across continents as well as overseas, and Bibles traveled with them.

In 1605 King James I commissioned an English translation of the Bible, gathering fifty-four of the leading scholars in England for the task.

It took six years to create what has been called one of the most profound literary and religious achievements in the English language. The King James Bible helped to shape a nation by a shared set of words and meanings. Within a hundred years, through the wide reading of that printed Bible, the English became one of the most literate populations in Europe. Benson Bobrick, author of *Wide as the Waters: The Story of the English Bible and the Revolution It Inspired*, a recent study of that Bible, suggests that "it sanctioned the right and capacity of people to think for themselves." It may even have led to the creation of modern democracy, he believes.

Among the separatist groups in England were the Puritans, who opposed the rites and discipline of the Church of England. They were mostly farmers and artisans. At their head was William Brewster. He led them to Holland in 1608, and there, at Leiden, he founded the Pilgrim Press, which issued some twenty religious books and tracts that were smuggled into England. We know the Puritans as the Pilgrims who sailed on the *Mayflower* in 1620 to found Plymouth Colony in Massachusetts.

When life in Holland proved difficult for several reasons, Brewster and his group decided to move to the New World. Brewster sailed on the *Mayflower* with his wife, two sons, and two boys who were indentured servants. An indentured servant is someone who agrees to work for a certain period of time, usually in exchange for travel expenses and room and board. Before landing, the Pilgrims signed an agreement providing for a government by the will of the majority. Called the Mayflower Compact, it was a step toward democracy.

TEN

The Printing Press and Democracy

Educated men were among the first immigrants to New England. Among them was Jesse Glover, a minister who soon returned to England to secure a printing press and a printer to run it. Matthew Day, an eighteen-year-old, accepted the job and moved to Massachusetts. In 1639 he set up the first press near Harvard, the college just established in Cambridge, Massachusetts.

From that press came the Bay Psalm Book, the earliest laws of the colony, many religious and scholarly works, and an Indian-language translation of the Bible. After some time other presses appeared—in Philadelphia, New York, Virginia, and Maryland. That printing expansion was slow is not surprising, for in the early 1700s the colonies had a population of scarcely 400,000, scattered over huge areas. The colonists read books, but most of them had been printed in England. American printers survived on routine work—government proclamations, laws and license forms, almanacs, alphabet primers, ship manifests and bills of lading, the sermons of local ministers, commercial leaflets, ballad broadsides, and prayer books.

Even these limited forms of printing were further restricted by the

JOHN PETER ZENGER'S PAPER, THE *WEEKLY JOURNAL*, CRITICAL OF NEW YORK'S COLONIAL GOVERNOR, IS BURNED BY BRITISH OFFICERS ON WALL STREET. A FEW YEARS LATER, ZENGER BECAME THE PUBLIC PRINTER FOR THE COLONIES OF NEW YORK AND NEW JERSEY.

colonial governors. They distrusted printers, feared criticism, and tried to censor their productions. But by 1763, print shops were firmly established in all thirteen colonies. And as greater freedom was secured, printers had a stronger hand in shaping public opinion. Most printers hoped to own a newspaper, and several succeeded. It was important because newspaper publishing, along with the printing of official documents, became the main source of prosperity for printers.

The colonists felt cut off, struggling to survive far from their homeland in thinly populated regions. The newspaper was what they looked to for news from everywhere. Though print runs were small, some 2,000 papers sprang up between 1690 and 1820. Only about a fifth of them lasted more than ten years.

The printer-journalist was often a one-man operation. He gathered and wrote the news, then printed and distributed it, almost always in close collaboration with the postmaster. In fact, some printers became postmasters, and vice versa. The printer's office served several functions: as a relay station for the mails, as a bookshop, and as a center of news and communication. By the end of the 1700s, a busy printing trade had been established, aided by a papermaking industry which freed it from dependence on European sources.

Some printers took an interest in literary life. They published poems, essays, stories, hymns, and letters. But by the 1750s the gathering storm over the colonies' relationship with England, the mother country, released a flood of political writing. Oratory, political satire, and verse took up many pages in newspapers as well as the magazines that some more enterprising printers had started.

Resistance to censorship was greatly strengthened through the fight waged by the New York printer John Peter Zenger from 1735 to 1736. Persecuted by the colonial governor, he was jailed and tried for libel. A jury refused to convict him, and news of his freedom made a great stir in all the colonies. Now printers knew freedom of speech and the press was not limited to the rich and powerful. Printing was at the heart of the ideas shaping the American Revolution.

In fact, the first best-seller in American history came off press on January 17, 1776. It was called *Common Sense*, and Thomas Paine was the author. Not a book, but a pamphlet, it quickly sold 150,000 copies. That was a huge number at a time when the most popular newspapers sold about 2,000 copies per week.

A poor English immigrant looking for a new start in life, Paine had settled in Philadelphia two years before. Siding with those colonists who wanted to break with Britain, his savage attack on England made brilliantly clear to Americans what they were against: the system of monarchy itself and its inequality. He called not only for independence, but also for the establishment of a republic— a representative form of government.

PORTRAIT OF THOMAS PAINE, PASSIONATE PAMPHLETEER

A writer who had both brains and passion, he produced one of the great gems of propaganda literature. In no time the demand for *Common Sense* exhausted the printers and presses of the colonies. Since the population of the colonies was only three million, with the pamphlet being passed from hand to hand and read aloud in public places, it seemed that just about every American had gotten the message. Paine convinced them that independence was desirable, was necessary, and was possible.

The pamphlet went through twenty-five editions in a single year. Newspapers from New Hampshire to Georgia reprinted its most biting paragraphs. Those who could not read had it read aloud to them.

It was smashing proof of the power of the printed word. No one before

COMMON SENSE:

ADDRESSED TO THE

INHABITANTS

OF

AMERICA,

On the following interesting

SUBJECTS.

I. Of the Origin and Design of Government in general, with concise Remarks on the English Constitution.

II. Of Monarchy and Hereditary Succession.

III. Thoughts on the present State of American Affairs.

IV. Of the present Ability of America, with some miscellaneous Reflections.

Written by an ENGLISHMAN.

By Thomas Paine

Man knows no Master save creating HEAVEN,
Or those whom choice and common good ordain.
THOMSON.

PHILADELPHIA, Printed
And Sold by R. BELL, in Third-Street, 1776.

TITLE PAGE OF THOMAS PAINE'S BEST-SELLING PAMPHLET

Paine had appealed to the common people—the farmers, artisans, small shopkeepers—who never sat in legislatures. These were the people who had to be convinced and aroused if the Revolution was to be won. Long afterward, the British historian George Trevelyan, writing a history of the American Revolution, said, "It would be difficult to name any human composition which has had an effect so extended and so lasting."

Reading *Common Sense* in camp, General George Washington declared it "sound doctrine and unanswerable reason." When an independence resolution was introduced in the Continental Congress, the delegates debated it and then appointed a committee to draft the Declaration of Independence. Thomas Jefferson, only thirty-three, was asked to draft it with the help of Benjamin Franklin and John Adams. Some changes were made by them and by the Congress, and on July 4, 1776, the declaration was adopted and printed.

The congressional printer, John Dunlap, was given the job of making up broadsides printed on one side of a sheet of heavy paper, suitable for posting on walls. Caslon was chosen as the typeface because it is clean and highly legible, and gives the impression of upright sturdiness. The broadsides were sent to all the colonies by couriers on horseback. They were posted and read aloud to the people in hundreds of assemblies in capitals, courthouses, pulpits, and town squares, and newspapers also published the text.

Many Voices

One of the ways in which the printing press expanded democracy was by giving even the poor a voice. Though born in poverty, Isaiah Thomas (1749–1831) became one of the most significant printers of his time. At sixteen he was apprenticed to a Boston printer for five years. For the next five he worked for printers in Nova Scotia, New Hampshire, the Carolinas, and Bermuda. In 1770, back in Boston, he launched the *Massachusetts Spy*, a popular paper that caused the king's loyalists to mark him as a troublemaker. He escaped their interference by shipping his press by wagon and at night to Worcester, Massachusetts.

ISAIAH THOMAS'S PRINTING PRESS WAS THE FIRST TO RECORD THE BATTLE OF CONCORD, ONE OF THE EARLY SKIR-
MISHES THAT SET THE COLONIES ON THE ROAD TO WAR WITH GREAT BRITAIN. DURING THE AMERICAN REVOLUTION,
THE PRINTING PRESS HELPED TO HASTEN THE SPREAD OF INFORMATION FROM REMOTE BATTLE SITES TO CITIES, TOWNS,
AND SEATS OF GOVERNMENT.

There he printed the first report of the revolution's bloody beginning at Lexington and Concord under the flaming headline: "Americans!—Liberty or Death!—Join or Die!"

With independence won, Thomas stayed in Worcester to build the most successful printing enterprise in the nation. It included print shops, newspapers, book publishing, bookstores, even a paper mill. One of Thomas's most passionate projects was his illustrated edition of the English Bible, the first to be published in America. He was determined to prove that American printing was every bit as good as the best England had to offer. His deluxe edition, with fifty copperplate illustrations that he had four New England artists create, appeared in 1791. Benjamin Franklin was one of many who hailed it as the most beautiful book produced in America.

Clifford K. Shipton, a biographer of Thomas, wrote:

> A great part of the American people learned their letters from his primers, got their news from his newspapers, sang from his hymnals, ordered their lives by his almanacs, and read his novels and Bibles. It was genius as well as opportunity which made him the first American capitalist of the printing business, for some of the rivals of his youth died in their old age in little one-room shops like that in which he began.

Today, what historians especially cherish Thomas for is his hobby—collecting materials about the history of printing. In Worcester, he founded the American Antiquarian Society, to which he donated many broadsides and posters gathered from all over America. It is an invaluable treasury for research into early American history.

Men were not alone in running printing presses. All the crafts and trades included at least a few women. They operated inns and taverns, managed fleets of ships, were blacksmiths, shipwrights, apothecaries, undertakers, even practiced law and medicine. When Ben Franklin's brother James died in Newport, Rhode Island, his widow kept his newspaper going. A Philadelphia woman, Lydia Bailey, ran her husband's print shop for thirty years after he died. She trained many apprentices, although all were male. At least six women served as official printers to provincial governments, and one of them, Ann Catherine Hoof Green, was the public printer for the city of Annapolis from 1767 to 1775. Women printers produced almanacs and books as well as newspapers.

And then there were gifted women such as Lydia Maria Child and Margaret Fuller who made historic advances for women in the newspaper world. In 1841, Child moved from Boston to New York to edit the *National Anti-Slavery Standard*—the first woman to edit a journal of public policy, and the first to syndicate a regular column on New York City life to other papers. At the beginning, Child was sneered at by the male press, but she won their respect when she dramatically increased the *Standard's* circulation.

LYDIA MARIA CHILD WAS A LEADER IN THE ANTISLAVERY MOVEMENT. HER WRITING AND EDITING GREATLY ENHANCED PUBLIC AWARENESS.

MARGARET FULLER, WHO BECAME FOREIGN CORRESPONDENT FOR THE *NEW-YORK TRIBUNE*, DIED AT SEA. SHE MADE HISTORIC STRIDES FOR WOMEN.

Margaret Fuller was an editor of the *Dial*, a literary magazine founded by Ralph Waldo Emerson in Concord. In 1844 Horace Greeley, editor of the *New-York Tribune,* asked her to move to New York to join his staff. He gave her free rein to write about whatever interested her—the arts, social reform, personalities. In 1846 he sent her to Italy as his foreign correspondent to cover the fight for an Italian republic. Four years later, on her way home with her family, she died in a shipwreck during a storm at sea.

A PORTRAIT OF BENJAMIN FRANKLIN, THE MOST PROLIFIC AND MOST ESTEEMED OF ALL THE COLONIAL PRINTERS

TWELVE

In Love with the Printed Word

A surprising number of Americans known for their eloquence and skill as writers started out as printers. Benjamin Franklin (1706–1790), who achieved fame as a scientist and a diplomat, worked at the craft of printing for many years. At the age of twelve he entered the trade in Boston, as apprentice to his half-brother James. Picture him in his deer-skin breeches, blue wool knit stockings, long-sleeved speckled shirt, and thick, well-greased shoes—the outfit worn by most printers' apprentices. He did the usual boy's chores while James struggled to hunt up new business. They printed with a wooden press developed by a Dutchman a hundred years earlier, a press that would not be outmoded until the coming of the iron press two centuries later. When James let him begin, Ben learned to set type from handwritten copy and then moved on to master the complex press. Printing was hard, slow work, but it was never dull to Ben. The two worked a twelve-hour day and often a few hours beyond that. Ben quickly became as expert as his brother. Printing was a craft he never tired of. Whether he was living in America, England, or France—the great capitals that he visited during his life as a diplomat for the American colonies—he would always have a press at hand. Great as his accomplishments were, when he wrote his last will, he

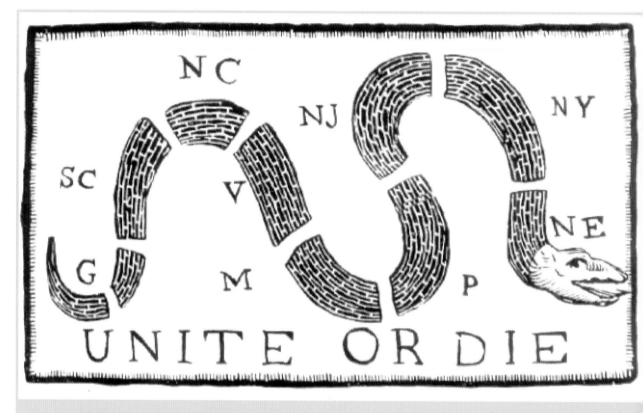

began it: "I, Benjamin Franklin, printer. . . ." He was a "leather apron man" (or, man of trade) in the slang of his day, was proud of it, and never forgot it.

In 1721, when Ben was fifteen, his brother decided to publish a newspaper, the *New England Courant*. There were already two such papers in Boston, but they served the stuffy establishment by publishing official orders and proclamations. Fresh news or ideas had no place in their pages. Poets, essayists, budding politicians, and social reformers had no outlet for their feelings and ideas. The *Courant*, only a single sheet printed on both sides, was opened to them. It printed satirical comments on local events and personalities and created news by working up sensational controversies. Ben added spice to the paper by creating Mrs. Silence Dogood, a busybody of a widow with a saucy pen. She was a hit.

But when the brothers quarreled, Ben ran off to the Quaker town of Philadelphia, where he found work on a weekly paper. Soon he was off to London to work in a huge shop that employed fifty printers. He stayed for eighteen months, then returned to Philadelphia, where he became foreman of a print shop. With his many skills he fashioned the molds for the types they needed and cast the types in lead. He also made the ink and the engravings and in short was, as he said, "quite a factotum."

Soon Franklin took over a young paper, the *Pennsylvania Gazette*. By 1729 he owned his press, the newspaper, and a shop selling supplies of many kinds, including books. His *Gazette* accepted ads for the sale of slaves, and sometimes bought slaves as an investment. But in the final stage of his long life he founded the Pennsylvania abolition society and became its president. His last political essay, written a month before he died, was an attack upon slavery.

The poet Walt Whitman also began his working life as a printer. Born in 1819 on Long Island, he grew up in what was then the village of Brooklyn, New York. His formal schooling ended at eleven. A year later the editor of a weekly paper, the *Long Island Patriot*, took him on as an apprentice. At that time such papers were mostly one-man operations, with a youngster like Walt around to do the drudgery and learn the trade.

It was good schooling for the boy, for such small-time publishers were both printer and reporter. Walt learned to set the type, run the press, and

At sixteen, Franklin printed out his ideas on what was important:

Without freedom of thought there can be no such thing as wisdom; and no such thing as public liberty, without freedom of speech, which is the right of every man, as far as by it, he does not hurt or control the right of another: and this the only check it ought to suffer, and the only bounds it ought to know.

WALT WHITMAN, ONE OF AMERICA'S GREATEST POETS, LEFT SCHOOL AT THE AGE OF ELEVEN TO START WORK AS AN APPRENTICE PRINTER. IN 1855, AT THE AGE OF THIRTY-SIX, HE HELPED PRINT THE FIRST EDITION OF HIS CLASSIC, *LEAVES OF GRASS*.

handle the business and editorial sides. That experience of a single person doing the whole job would influence Walt when it came time for him to publish the many editions of his classic, *Leaves of Grass.*

Over the next several years he found work with other printers in Brooklyn, on Long Island, and in Manhattan. On these small papers a few of his first writings got into print anonymously. At seventeen he began to take teaching jobs in various Long Island towns, but in 1841 went back to work as printer for newspapers. He wrote articles and editorials for some, but began to turn to poetry to capture the emotions and imaginations of Americans, the people he loved. He crafted a poetry that would break all bounds. He published his masterpiece, *Leaves of Grass,* in 1855, the first of the seven constantly expanding editions he would create before his death in 1892.

Sam Clemens, who became famous under the pen name Mark Twain (1835–1910), grew up in the Mississippi River town of Hannibal, Missouri. He was apprenticed to a printer at the age of thirteen. It was a small print shop, publishing the *Missouri Courier* as well as taking on jobs for individual clients. An apprentice worked for bed and board, two suits per year—and no wages. The bed was a mattress on the shop floor, and first suit was a hand-me-down that fitted like a circus tent. He never got the second suit. The board (food) was so pitiful that he stole potatoes from the boss's cellar and cooked them secretly on the office stove.

He worked hard at becoming a capable and swift journeyman printer. Always ready to learn something new, he soon moved up to subeditor. He liked the smell of printer's ink. As it had been for Ben Franklin, the print shop became the "poor boy's college" for the man later known as Mark Twain.

When his older brother Orion left St. Louis and returned to Hannibal to start a new weekly paper, Clemens quit his apprenticeship and joined him to work as a printer and editorial assistant. Orion promised him $3.50 a week, "an extravagant wage," Twain later said, "but it cost him nothing, for he was never able to pay me a single penny." At least Clemens could sleep under his mother's roof, and he enjoyed working alongside his younger brother Henry, later apprenticed to Orion as well.

SAMUEL CLEMENS, ONE OF AMERICA'S MOST BELOVED AUTHORS, BECAME A PRINTER'S APPRENTICE AT THE AGE OF THIRTEEN. HE WORKED AT HIS CRAFT AT SEVERAL NEWSPAPERS BEFORE WINNING FAME AS A NOVELIST KNOWN UNIVERSALLY AS MARK TWAIN.

At fifteen, Clemens wrote his first humorous piece, which was published in Orion's newspaper. During his three years with Orion he wrote other funny pieces. Then, at eighteen, Clemens left home to try his luck in the world beyond. He worked in the composing room of papers in St. Louis, Philadelphia, New York, and Iowa; became a journalist, a writer of popular tall tales, and the author of the enormously popular classic novel *Huckleberry Finn*, among many others.

The Power of Print

Born a slave in Maryland in 1818, Frederick Douglass escaped to freedom and by an iron will, hard work, and great talent helped to win his people's freedom. His magnificent speeches and his brilliant writing made him one of the great men of nineteenth-century America. His life illustrates the power of print in helping to break the chains of slavery.

Many Northerners learned what slavery was like when former slaves like Douglass began to tell their stories in print. The details of their lives in bondage carried a powerful antislavery message.

By law, custom, and popular prejudice, slaves in the South (and in the North, too) were not allowed to learn to read. As a youngster in Baltimore, working as a house slave, Douglass was taught to read by a sympathetic mistress. Her husband quickly put a stop to the "crime," however, declaring that reading would spoil even the best black, "forever unfitting him for the duties of a slave."

The boy went on learning secretly, teaching himself out of his only book, Noah Webster's elementary spelling book. Then, at twelve, he bought his own copy of the *Columbian Orator*, a collection of patriotic speeches and a handbook on oratory. In the book was a dialogue

FREDERICK DOUGLASS, THE FUGITIVE SLAVE WHO BECAME ONE OF THE FOREMOST FIGHTERS FOR HIS PEOPLE'S FREEDOM, MASTERED THE POWER OF WORDS BOTH IN ORATORY AND IN PRINT.

between a master and his slave. The master makes a case for slavery while the slave eloquently justifies his right to rebel and run away. Here young Frederick found the words for the thought he had not yet been able to articulate. This one book made an enormous difference in his life. At the age of twenty-one he fled slavery and in the years ahead, as lecturer, editor, writer, organizer, and diplomat, he earned the leadership of the African Americans in their struggle to emancipate themselves.

An interesting sidelight on the power of the printed word on people not allowed to learn to read comes out of studies of the Denmark Vesey slave conspiracy of 1822, in Charleston, South Carolina. Vesey, after many years as a slave, bought his freedom when he won a $1,500 lottery and established his own carpentry business. Using church meetings as a cover, he planned a slave insurrection. One of his recruiting methods was to read to his followers the speeches of the antislavery senators from the transcripts of the great debate in Congress over whether to permit slavery in Missouri.

Betrayed by informers, Vesey was hanged along with thirty-four other men.

William Lloyd Garrison (1805–1879), was a printer-editor who would one day publish Frederick Douglass's slave narrative and rise to leadership in the abolition movement. He was born in Newburyport, Massachusetts, and at twelve, was apprenticed for a term of seven years to the editor and owner of the local paper.

Printing was a trade he loved. Quickly he mastered composition of type, the makeup of pages, and the operation of the printing press. An older co-worker taught the teenager Latin and started him reading English and American literature. Going into the fourth year of his apprenticeship, Garrison wrote an unsigned letter to the editor that was so lively that the paper printed it. It was only the first of several pieces to be published after his identity was discovered. They ranged over so many different subjects that Garrison himself was amazed that someone with as little formal

William Lloyd Garrison, apprenticed at the age of twelve at a Massachusetts newspaper, would found and edit *The Liberator*, one of the most powerful antislavery publications.

THE LIBERATOR.

VOL. I.]

WILLIAM LLOYD GARRISON AND ISAAC KNAPP, PUBLISHERS.

[NO. 17.

BOSTON, MASSACHUSETTS.]   OUR COUNTRY IS THE WORLD—OUR COUNTRYMEN ARE MANKIND.   [SATURDAY, APRIL 23, 1831.

THE LIBERATOR

IS PUBLISHED WEEKLY

AT NO. 11, MERCHANTS' HALL.

WM. LLOYD GARRISON, EDITOR.

TERMS.

Two Dollars per annum, payable in advance.

Agents allowed every sixth copy.

No subscription will be received for a shorter period than six months.

All letters and communications must be POST PAID.

AGENTS.

CHARLES WHIPPLE, *Newburyport, Mass.*
JAMES E. ELLIS, *Providence, R. I.*
PHILIP A. BELL, *New-York City.*
JOSEPH CASSEY, *Philadelphia, Pa.*
HENRY OGDEN, *Newark, N. J.*
WILLIAM WATKINS, *Baltimore, Md.*

THE LIBERATOR.

' Is not the plea, that emancipation is impracticable, the most impudent hypocrisy and the most glaring absurdity ever propounded for contemplation?—Can any suppositious expediency, any dread of political disorder, or any private advantage, justify the prolongation of corruption, the enormity of which is unequalled, or repel the holy claim to its extinction? The system is so entirely corrupt, that it admits of no cure but by a TOTAL and IMMEDIATE abolition. For a gradual emancipation is a virtual recognition of the right, and establishes the rectitude of the practice. If it be just for one moment, it is hallowed for ever; and it be inequitable, not a day should it be tolerated.'

BOURNE.

two committee men and a constable interfered, and would not permit him to take his seat! He was finally driven away, and the pew passed into other hands.

We purpose shortly to visit all our meeting-houses, and ascertain what places are provided for the accommodation of our colored people. A house dedicated to the worship of Almighty God, should be the last place for the exercise of despotic principles.—But here is the extract:

' With deep regret we have observed some articles in the columns of the " Liberator," of Boston, apparently from this city, in which its inhabitants are implicated; and which we believe the editor of that publication will deem very injudicious, as well as unkind, when knowing the truth in the case. So far from wishing to deprive the colored population of an opportunity to worship God, by the co-operation of the friends of religion with that part of the inhabitants, a good and convenient house was erected a few years since; clergymen of different denominations have often officiated, gratuitously, from Sabbath to Sabbath; and when disappointed in the labors of a Minister, lay brethren have attended at their request, and made exertions to promote the prosperity of their congregation; for many years a Sabbath School has been taught, composed entirely of colored children and adults; in addition to this, if we mistake not, at their request the public school money is given them in proportion to the number of their children, and they thus have a day school of their own.

After such interest had been shown for that class of people, was it to be expected that an attack should be made upon the very persons who have shown such liberality? This is indeed gratifying to the enemies of benevolent exertions; and were the

be elevated and improved in this country; unanimous in opposing their instruction; unanimous in exciting the prejudices of the people against them; unanimous in apologising for the crime of slavery; unanimous in conceding the right of the planters to hold their slaves in a limited bondage; unanimous in denying the expediency of emancipation, unless the liberated slaves are sent to Liberia; unanimous in their hollow pretence for colonizing, namely, to evangelize Africa; unanimous in their *true motive* for the measure—a terror lest the blacks should rise to avenge their accumulated wrongs. It is a conspiracy to send the free people of color to Africa under a benevolent pretence, but really that the slaves may be held more securely in bondage. It is a conspiracy based upon fear, oppression and falsehood, which draws its aliment from the prejudices of the people, which is sustained by duplicity, which is impotent in its design, which really upholds the slave system, which fascinates while it destroys, which endangers the safety and happiness of the country, which no precept of the bible can justify, which is implacable in its spirit, which should be annihilated at a blow.

These are our accusations; and if we do not substantiate them, we are willing to be covered with reproach.

In attacking the principles, and exposing the evil tendency of the Society, we wish no one to understand us as saying, that all its friends are equally guilty, or actuated by the same motives. Nor let him suppose, that we exonerate any of them from

virtue. I doubt not this conviction will ultimately prevail in every community, where the obligations of religion and philanthropy are acknowledged; though the process may be slow; having to contend with much ignorance prejudice and error. This conviction, however, is but the first step towards a result so desirable as the total abolition of slavery. Every long established custom acquires a strong hold on the feelings of those who are habituated to its control; we know that its power in many cases is almost unconquerable; and this is especially the case, where a custom, however injurious in its tendencies, is a source of pecuniary emolument, or worldly aggrandizement to those interested in its continuance. It therefore becomes necessary for the attainment of this great and good object—the universal emancipation of our colored brethren—the complete overthrow of this abominable traffic in human flesh—to investigate the whole subject fairly and calmly; to discuss it fully and freely; to ascertain, as far as possible, what are the best means and methods for the accomplishment of this great end. On this point, I find there is great diversity of opinion. Men of equal talents, equal piety, and equal benevolence, take different and almost opposite views of the whole subject: my mind has been much perplexed, by hearing what seemed to me very strong arguments on both sides of the question.

With regard to the main subject, universal emancipation, as I before remarked, I have no doubt. I think it may, and it ought to be accomplished; but with regard to the means of its accomplishment, I do not feel so decided. I as...

THE FRONT PAGE OF AN EARLY ISSUE OF WILLIAM LLOYD GARRISON'S WEEKLY NEWSPAPER.

education as he had could effectively address such a variety of topics.

At twenty, Garrison began to move from one printing and editing job to another. Gradually he developed into a universal reformer, a kind of moral legislator who believed many things were wrong and felt that he had to do something about it. In his papers he campaigned against what he saw as evils: alcohol, wife-beating, theatergoing, dancing, dueling, gambling, swearing, prostitution, imprisonment for debt—and slavery. No doubt he was influenced by the exciting atmosphere of Boston, where so many reforms were born.

After still more job-shifting, Garrison, at the age of twenty-five, found what he was born for. He launched one of the most remarkable ventures in the history of journalism, *The Liberator*. It was a newspaper that would fight unrelentingly for an immediate and unconditional end to slavery. It appeared weekly without missing an issue for thirty-five years, ceasing publication only when the Thirteenth Amendment to the Constitution ended slavery in December 1865.

With only a font of worn, secondhand type rescued from a foundry, a well-worn press, and a one-room print shop in a Boston building, Garrison and one helper set the type, composed the eight pages, performed the presswork, folded, bundled, and mailed the papers, handled the correspondence, and, of course, wrote much of the contents.

He succeeded in reaching both black and white readers, in building antislavery societies, and in shaping opinion and winning supporters to the cause both among the public and in the halls of Congress. He attacked not only slavery but the racial prejudice and political hypocrisy that sustained it. As he swore in his first issue:

I am in earnest—I will not equivocate—I will not excuse—
I will not retreat a single inch—AND I WILL BE HEARD.

CRAFTSMEN AT WORK IN THE LITHOGRAPHY SECTION OF A PRINT SHOP, AROUND 1885

The New Place of Print

It was during the decades leading up to the American Revolution that another revolution was in the making—the Industrial Revolution. The Western world was moving from a stable agricultural society to a modern industrial society. Dramatic changes in social and economic life took place as inventions and technological advances created the factory system of large-scale production and greater economic specialization. Working people began moving into the growing urban centers.

Printing, too, was reshaped by these forces. With the growth of the iron trade, the use of the centuries-old wooden press gave way in 1772 to a new press, developed in Basel, Switzerland. Now all parts that were subject to stress were made of iron. In 1798 the Englishman Earl Stanhope made the next advance—a press made entirely of iron.

That same year, however, an even more remarkable advance occurred. Aloys Senefelder, a German playwright, reported that after two years of work he had succeeded in inventing lithography. Founded on the basic idea that grease and water do not mix, it revolutionized printing. In his early experiments he etched in relief onto pieces of stone containing lime. But he soon found that pure limestone—which absorbs grease and water—would overcome the need to work that way. He drew on the limestone in reverse with a greasy crayon, a weak solution of nitric acid, and gum arabic, and dampened the stone. The water stuck only to the parts that were not covered by the greasy design. Next, he inked the stone, and the ink only stuck to the design. He then pressed the paper against the stone and transferred the image to paper. Soon the process was adapted so that metal plates could be used.

For years another German, Friedrich Koenig, worked on creating a power press. Finally, in 1812, he built a steam-operated twin-cylinder machine. Within two years the *Times* of London was printing its newspapers with it. The new machine produced 1,100 sheets an hour, four times more than the old manually operated press had done.

Those two innovations—lithography and the power press—combined to lower the cost of printing and thereby to widen the market for it. Printing was now altogether more affordable. In 1833 a New York newspaper, the *Sun*, was able to drop its price to a penny a copy. Cheaper books and newspapers meant the pleasure and value of reading were no longer confined to the upper classes.

Still other technological changes further speeded the advance of the printing industry. An engineer in France made important improvements in papermaking machinery. His design formed the basis for the modern manufacture of paper. Richard Hoe, a New York engineer, applied the principle of rotary motion to the cylinder press in 1846. The Walter press was able to print on a continuous roll of paper and the Eichhoff press could print two sides simultaneously. In 1886 Ottmar Mergenthaler invented the linotype machine, so that movable type could be created by machine instead of by hand. It speeded up production remarkably.

There were other advances in the complex process that affected not only productivity but the living standards of the men and women who did the work. Wages improved and so did working conditions. Prices became stabilized. Printers who did jobbing work (hired on a project by project basis) were more and more in demand, and so were newspaper printers.

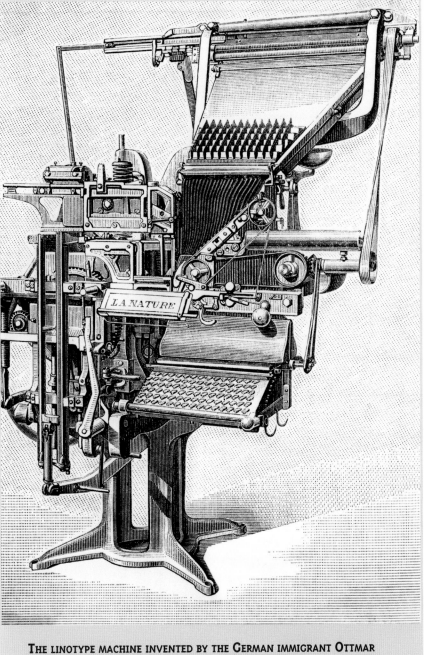

THE LINOTYPE MACHINE INVENTED BY THE GERMAN IMMIGRANT OTTMAR
MERGENTHALER AND PUT INTO USE IN 1886 AT THE *NEW-YORK TRIBUNE*

CHESTER CARLSON WITH THE FIRST MODEL OF HIS INVENTION,
THE PHOTOCOPIER

Photography, invented by the Frenchman Louis Daguerre in 1839, began to reach the public press through the photoengraving process. By 1871 it was commercially practiced for letterpress printing. And by 1880 photoengraved prints were replacing woodcuts as illustrations in books, magazines, and newspapers. The first halftones were black and white. Later, color-process work was introduced.

As the twentieth century wore on, inventions seemed to know no bounds. Many innovations influenced the place of print in our culture: the typewriter, the photocopier, photomechanical composition, cathode-ray tubes, and laser technologies. To make documents in print available to everyone, along came the photocopier. Word processing reshaped editing and offered more flexibility to the writing process. Computer printing? It's hard to keep up with the stream of innovation in the process.

The Internet and interactive multimedia have added new dimensions to the role of print. Perhaps it's too soon to forecast the cultural impact of all this ongoing change. Surely it will continue to reshape the way we humans connect with one another.

Afterword

Printing, as we have seen, has been a great force in the course of history. Knowledge, religion, science, politics, and culture were all transformed by the possibilities of the printed word. Printing materials were used in every way the imagination could conceive. The almost boundless reach of identical texts and images shapes the way we live. In this age of worldwide networks employing technologies that seem to change continuously, it may be helpful to understand how it began. And to think about where it may go.

The Great Idea Finder: The Printing Press
http://www.ideafinder.com/history/inventions/story039.htm

Printing: History and Development
http://www.digitalcentury.com/encyclo/update/print.html

Bibliography

Amory, Hugh, and David D. Hall, eds., *A History of the Book in America, vol. I, The Colonial Book in the Atlantic World*. New York: Cambridge University Press, 2000.

Barzun, Jacques. *From Dawn to Decadence: 500 Years of Western Cultural Life, 1500 to the Present*. New York: HarperCollins, 2000.

Basbanes, Nicolas A. *A Gentle Madness: Bibliophiles, Bibliomanes, and the Eternal Passion for Books*. New York: Henry Holt & Company, l995.

Bernal, J.D. *Science in History*. London: Watts, 1854.

Boas, Marie. *The Scientific Renaissance 1450–1630*. New York: Harper, 1962.

Bobrick, Benson. *Wide as the Waters: The Story of the English Bible and the Revolution It Inspired*. New York: Simon & Schuster, 2001.

Bode, Carl. *The Anatomy of American Popular Culture, 1840–1861*. Berkeley: University of California Press, 1959.

Boorstin, Daniel J. *The Creators*. New York: Random House, 1992.

———. *The Seekers*. New York: Random House, 1998.

Braudel, Fernand. *The Wheels of Commerce*. New York: Harper & Row, 1982.

Bruno, Leonard C. *The Tradition of Technology: Landmarks of Western Technology in the Collection of the Library of Congress*. Washington: Library of Congress, 1995.

Burke, Peter. *A Social History of Knowledge: From Gutenberg to Diderot*. Malden, England: Blackwell, 2000.

Burrows, Edwin G., and Mike Wallace. *Gotham: A History of New York City to 1898*. New York: Oxford University Press, 2001.

Crystal, David. *The Cambridge Encyclopedia of the English Language*. New York: Cambridge University Press, 1995.

Davies, Norman. *Europe: A History*. New York: Oxford University Press, 1996.

Diamond, Jared. *Guns, Germs and Steel: The Fates of Human Societies*. New York: W. W. Norton, 1997.

Donnelly, Daniel. *Upload: Taking Print to the Web*. Gloucester, MA: Rockport, 1998.

Eisenstein, Elizabeth L. *Printing Press as an Agent of Change*. New York: Cambridge University Press, 1979.

_____. *The Printing Revolution in Early Modern Europe*. New York: Cambridge University Press, 1984.

Febvre, Lucien, and Henri-Jean Martin. *The Coming of the Book: The Impact of Printing 1450–1800*. New York: Verso, 2000.

Furnas, J. C. *The Americans: A Social History of the United States 1587–1914*. New York: Putnam, 1969.

Hale, John. *The Civilization of Europe in the Renaissance*. New York: Touchstone, 1993.

Johns, Adrian. *The Nature of the Book: Print and Knowledge in the Making*. Chicago: University of Chicago Press, 1998.

Jones, Jacqueline. *American Work: Four Centuries of Black and White Labor*. New York: W. W. Norton, 1998.

Landes, David S. *The Wealth and Poverty of Nations*. New York: W. W. Norton, 1998.

Larkin, Jack. *The Reshaping of Everyday Life: 1790–1840*. New York: HarperCollins, 1988.

Lee, Marshall. *Bookmaking: The Illustrated Guide to Design and Production*. New York: Brewster, 1976.

Martin, Henri-Jean. *The History and Power of Writing*. Chicago: University of Chicago Press, 1994.

Pollard, Michael. *Johann Gutenberg: Master of Modern Printing*. Woodbridge, CT: Blackbirch, 1992.

Rostenberg, Leona, and Madeline Stern. *Old Books, Rare Friends: Two Literary Sleuths and Their Shared Passion*. New York: Doubleday, 1993.

Spiller, Robert, ed., *Literary History of the United States*. New York: Macmillan, 1963.

Wilson, Adrian. *The Design of Books*. Salt Lake City: Peregrine Smith, 1974.

Index

Page numbers in **boldface** are illustrations.

Aldine Press, 52
Alexander the Great, 21
alphabet, 14
American Antiquarian Society, 86
art, **10**, **12**, 13
     See also illustrations
artists, 41, 51
astronomy, 54, **68**
authors, 31, 52, 54, **90**, 91–93,
     94, 95, **96**, 97
See also journalists; poets

Bailey, Lydia, 87
Banks, Sir Joseph, **66**, 67
Baskerville, William, 45
Bibles, 21, 35, 37, **38**, 45, 47,
     51, **74–75**, 76–77, 78, 86
Blaue, Willem, 73
Boccaccio, 31

Bodoni, Giambattista, 45
Bomberg, Daniel, 71
books
    in antiquity, 18, **19**, **20**, 21–23
    in the Middle Ages, 23, 29, 31, 42, **42**,
       43, **44**, 45
     See also scrolls
bookstores, 22, 63
Brewster, William, 77
broadsheets, 64
brotherhoods, 61

Carlson, Chester, **108**
cartoons, 51, 71, **92**
Caslon, William, 45
Catherine the Great, 71
Caxton, William, **42**, 42–43, **44**, 45
Chaucer, Geoffrey, 43, **44**
Child, Lydia Maria, 87, **87**

China, 15, 23, 25, 25, 26–27, **26**, 29, 71, 72

clay tablets, **13**, 72

Clemens, Samuel, 95–97, **96**

Cleopatra, 21

codices (codex), 22

color, 71, 109

Columbus, Christopher, **40**, 41

columnists, 87, 93

commerce, 14, 29, 72

computers, 109

convents, 47, 49

Cook, James, 67

cookbooks, **50**, 51

Copernicus, Nicolaus, **68**, 69

copying, 21, 22, 23, **24–25**, 29, 61, 63, 67
See also counterfeiting; monasteries; photocopiers

copyrights, 65

counterfeiting, 47, 65

cuneiform writing, **13**, 15

Daguerre, Louis, 109

Dead Sea Scrolls, 22

democracy, **76**, 77

dictionaries, 54

Diderot, Denis, 63, **64**

Douglass, Frederick, 98, **99**, 100

editing, 63, 109

Egypt, ancient, **12**, 14, 15, 16, 18, **19**, **20**, 21, 72

Eichhoff press, 106

eighteenth century, 78, **79**, 80–81, **81**, **82**, 83–84, **84–85**, 86–87

Elzevier Press, 47

England, 42–43, **42**, **44**, 45, 54, 72, 76–77, 105

engraving, 26–27, 29, 39

Erasmus, **53**, 54

Europe, 21, 23, **24–25**, **28**, 29, 31, 33

explorers, **40**, 41, **66**, 67, 69, 72

fifteenth century, **32**, 33, 35, **36**, 36–37, **38**, 39, **40**, 41–43, **42**, **44**, 45

Florence, Italy, 41

fonts, 45

Franklin, Benjamin, 83, 86, **90**, 91–93

Franklin, James, 86–87, 91–93

Fuller, Margaret, 87, **88**, 89

Fust, Johann, 35, 37

Garrison, William Lloyd, 100, **101**, **102**, 103

Glover, Jesse, 78

Greeks (ancient), 16, 18, 21, 29, 49, 52, 69, 72

Green, Ann Catherine Hoof, 87

Gutenberg, Johann, 33, **34**, 35–37, **36**, **38**, 39

hieroglyphics, **15**, 15–16

Hoe, Richard, 106

how-to manuals, **50**, 51

humanists, 31, 54

hymns, 37

ideograms, 15, 16, 27, 71

illuminations, 31

illustrations, 39, **50**, 51, 67, **74–75**, 86

Industrial Revolution, 105–106

italics, 45, 52

Ivan the Terrible, 71

James I, 76

Japan, 71

Jenson, Nicolas, 45

Jesuits, 47, 71

Jews, 69, 71

journalists, 80, **84–85**, 84, 86, **88**, 88–89, 95, **96**, 97, 100, **101**, **102**, 103

Koenig, Friedrich, 106

Korea, 27, **27**

labor strikes, 61

libraries, **20**, 21–22, 47

linear B, 16

linotype machine, 106, **107**

lithography, **104**, 105–106

Luther, Martin, 45, **46**, 75

magazines, 80

Manutius, Aldus, 52, **52**, 61

maps, 69, 72–73, **73**

Mayflower Compact, **76**, 77

Medicis, 41

Mercator, Gerardus, 73

Mergenthaler, Otto, 106, **107**

Mesopotamia, **13**, 14, 15

metal, 27, 36–37, 105, 106

Middle Ages

    in China and Korea, **26**, 26–27, **27**

    in Europe, 21, 23, **24–25**, **28**, 29, **30**, 31, **32**, 33, 41

Middle East (ancient), **13**, 14, 15

monasteries, 23, **24–25**

    See also Jesuits

multimedia, 109

museums, 39, 86

Native Americans, **15**, 15–16, 78

newspapers, **79**, 80, 86–87, 92–93, **102**, 103, 106

nineteenth century, 73, 87, 89, **104**, 105–106, **107**

    See also Industrial Revolution

numbers, 14, 16

Ortelius, Abraham, 73, **73**

Paine, Thomas, **81**, 81, 83, **82**

Paleolithic period, 11, 13, **13**

palm leaves, 15

paper, 23, 25, 26, 80, 106

papyrus, **12**, 15, 16–17, 18, **19**, 22–23

parchment, 23

patronage, 31, 35, 54

peddlers, **58**, 63–64

pens, **12**, 16

Peter the Great, **70**, 71, 72

Petrarch, Francesco, **30**, 31, 52

Philip II, 51–52, 72

phonemics, 14, 16

photocopiers, **108**, 109

photoengraving, 109

photography, 109

Pilgrims, **76**, 77

Plantin, Christopher, 51–52

playing cards, **28**, 29, **62**

Polo, Marco, 29

popular literature, 29, 51

power press, 106

prehistoric times, **10**, 13, 26

press runs, 63, 106

printers

    fifteenth century, **32**, 33, 35, **36**, 36–37, **38**, 39, **40**, 41–43, **42**, **44**, 45

    eighteenth century, 78, **79**, 80–81, 84, **84–85**, 86, 87, **90**, 91–93

    nineteenth century, **94**, 95, **96**, 100, **101**, **102**, 103, 106

    seventeenth century, **58**, 78

    sixteenth century, 45, **48**, 49, 51–52, **52**, 59–61, 63

printing presses (mechanics of), **34**, 35–37, **48**, 105–106, **107**, 109

print shops

    American, 78, 80, 84, 86, 93, 95, 103, 105–106

    European, 41–42, **42**, **48**, 49, 51–52, 59–61, **60**, 105–106

propaganda, 76, 81

Puritans, **76**, 77

Reformation, 45, **46**, 47

religion, 15–16, 21, 26, 29, 35, 37, 42, 45, 47, 51–52, 64, 69, 71, **74–75**, 75–77, 78

    See also Bibles; Luther, Martin; monasteries

Renaissance, 29, **30**, 31, 41

Romans (ancient), 21–23, 31

Russia, **70**, 71, 72

science, 67, 69, **68**

scribes, 16, 22–23, **24–25**, 29, 45, 67

script, 39

scrolls, 16–17, 18, **19**, **20**, 22

Senefelder, Aloys, 105

seventeenth century, 63, 72, **76**, 77–78

Shakespeare, William, 54–55, **56**, 57

sixteenth century, 45, **46**, 47, **48**, 49, **50**,

51–52, **52–53**, 54–55, **56**, 57,
59–61, 67, **68**, 69,71–72, 75, 76
slavery, 42, 87, 93, 98, **99**, 100, **101**, **102**, 103
Smith, William, 73
social reformers, 87, 89, **99**, 100, **101**, 103
sounds (representation of), 14, 16
Stanhope, Earl, 105
syndication, 87

Thomas, Isaiah, 84–85, 84, 86
time, 16
travel books, 31, **40**, 72
Twain, Mark, 95–97, **96**
     See also Clemens, Samuel
twentieth century, 73, 109
typefaces, 45
typesetting, **34**

United States
     Civil War, 98, **99**, 100, **101**, **102**,
     103
     early printers, 78, **79**, 80, 84,
     84–85, 86, 87, **90**, 91–93
     newspapers, **79**, 80, 84, **84–85**, 86,
     87, **88**, 89, 92, 93, 95, **101**, **102**,
     103
     paper, 80
     Revolutionary War, 78, **79**, 80, **81**,
     82, 83, 84, **84–85**, 86, **92**
     social reformers, 87, **87**, **88**, 89,

98, **99**, 100, **101**, **102**, 103
universities, 23, 29, 78

Venice, Italy, 52, **52**, 69, 70
vernacular, 29
Vesey, Denmark, 100

Walter press, 106
Web sites, 113
Whitman, Walt, 93, 95, **94**
women, 49, 59, **64**, 86–87, **87**, **88**, 89
woodcuts, **26**, 27, 39, **40**, 71, 109
writing, 11, **12**, **13**, 14, 15, **15**, 15–16, 18,
     21–23, **24–25**, 25, 27, 29, 67

Zenger, John Peter, **79**, 80

About the Author

Milton Meltzer has published more than one hundred books for young people and adults in the fields of history, biography and social issues. He has written or edited for newspapers, magazines, radio, television, and films.

In 2001 the American Library Association honored him with the Laura Ingalls Wilder Award for lifetime contributions to children's literature. Among his other honors are five nominations for the National Book Award as well as the Regina, Christopher, Jane Addams, Carter G. Woodson, Jefferson Cup, Washington Book Guild, Olive Branch, and Golden Kite awards. Many of his books have been chosen for the honor lists of the American Library Association, the National Council of Teachers of English, and the National Council for the Social Studies, as well as for *The New York Times* Best Books of the Year list.

Meltzer and his wife, Hildy, live in New York City. He is a member of the Authors Guild, American PEN, and the Organization of American Historians.